MICRO-CHURCH REVOLUTION!

The Complete Guide to Starting and Growing a Micro-Church

Rick Vincent

Just the WORD Publishing

THE MICRO-CHURCH REVOLUTION

Copyright © 2019 Rick Vincent

All rights reserved.

Published by:

Just the WORD Publishing
P.O. Box 350833
Palm Coast, FL 32135-9998 USA

No part of this publication may be reproduced, stored in a retrieval system or transmitted in any form or by any means without the prior written permission of the copyright owner. The scanning, uploading and distribution or redistribution of this book or eBook via the Internet or via any other means without the permission of the copyright owner is illegal and punishable by law. Your support of this author's rights is appreciated.

ISBN 978-0-9980464-0-2

Printed in the United States of America

Printed by CreateSpace, An Amazon.com Company

Available on Kindle

DEDICATION

To My Mom

Thank you for giving me a few of your many talents. May God bless you and keep you always.

"The Lord bless thee, and keep thee: The Lord make his face shine upon thee, and be gracious unto thee: The Lord lift up his countenance upon thee, and give thee peace."

(Numbers 6:24-26 KJV)

SPECIAL THANKS

To my gifted teachers Pastor Derek Sheavly, Daniel Murray, Andrew Wommack (awmi.net), Dr. Larry Hutton (larryhutton.org) and others who helped to accelerate the spiritual maturity process for me. To the passionate and stylish Pastor Jim Raley (calvaryfl.com) for his constant motivation.

Many thanks to those who helped with the book including Kathy, Chris, and Nick. Eternal thanks to my wife, Jenny, for her help with the book and for having faith in me. Utmost thanks to my Lord Jesus Christ for those middle-of-the-night downloads and step-by-step guidance.

"Let your light so shine before men, that they may see your good works, and glorify your Father which is in heaven."

(Matthew 5:16 KJV)

FREE BONUS!

MICRO-CHURCH STARTUP CHECKLIST

A quick-reference guide showing all of the steps needed to start a micro-church. Download this free checklist by clicking on the following link:

micro-churchrevolution.com/checklist

CONTENTS

1 Christianity Today 1
2 The Micro-Church 7
3 Sure Foundation 15
4 Revolutionary Instrument 23
5 Full Commitment 27
6 God's Master Plan 37
7 Divine Purpose 49
8 Core Beliefs 53
9 Community Formation 59
10 Disciple Development 69
11 Member Demographics 75
10 Member Contributions 79
13 Venue Selection 85
14 Worship Service Design 93
15 Important Observances 101
16 Breaking Bread 105
17 Legal Framework 109
18 Resource Requirements 115
19 Mission Design 121
20 Mission Promotion 129
21 Startup Process 135
22 Progress Evaluation 141
23 Averting Mistakes 147
24 Network Building 153
25 Church Planting 163
26 Revolution Ahead 175

PREFACE

"Let not your heart be troubled: ye believe in God, believe also in me." (John 14:1 KJV)

Christianity is at a crossroads...the Body of Christ is facing game-changing times. America, founded on Christian principles, is on the verge of becoming a post-Christian nation. God is being pushed out of every aspect of society. Non-believers are throwing everything they have into a campaign to discredit and destroy organized religion. Satan is orchestrating an attack that will jeopardize the very fabric of modern Christian life.

Inside the Church, believers are being driven out by legalistic doctrines and power-grabbing politics. Many worshipers are on the verge of leaving after years of dedicated service. Long-time members are so dissatisfied that abandoning the Christian community entirely appears to be the only option.

Young adults have earned the title of the "un-Christian generation." Many are shunning religion despite a lifetime family history of engagement. Aging demographics are putting some congregations at risk of extinction.

Millions of Christians in the United States are not even attending church. Some have left the Church and vowed never to return after bad experiences. Many followers have been on the sidelines for years waiting for the right opportunity to reengage. Others never fully committed to Christ even though they maintain to be of Christian faith.

Countless persons are searching for a new and exciting way to serve God but have not found the right connection. Religion and misguided doctrines have stood in the way of believers finding God's purpose for their lives. The unlimited potential represented by disconnected Christians is astounding.

Years of assault on all fronts have left the Church in disarray, but not without hope. Great things are still happening within the Body of Christ. Christians are joining forces to turn the tide despite the seemingly insurmountable odds.

The battle to retake our nation is in its infancy. Leading the way is a transformation of the Christian Church. Micro-churches are well positioned to play a key role in the revival currently being orchestrated from above.

Followers of Christ can no longer sit on the sidelines watching the Church struggle. Now is the time for all believers to join the battle. The crusade at hand will completely revolutionize the landscape of the Church. Help to shape the Church of the future by joining the micro-church revolution today!

The *Micro-Church Revolution* was written to reengage believers not currently attending church. This book provides the framework from within which Christians can regain their faith and fulfill God's plan for their life. The objectives of the book are to:

- Build a platform on which sidelined Christians can be reunited with the Body of Christ.
- Fill the gap for believers who are leaving traditional churches.
- Provide comprehensive resources for starting, growing, and expanding micro-churches.
- Facilitate the networking of micro-churches.
- Initiate a worldwide platform where micro-churches, traditional churches, and other organizations can collaborate and thrive.
- Empower micro-church networks to achieve great works for Christ.

- Ignite a revolution that will inspire traditional churches to "reboot" and make God and His Word the center of the Church.

In 2016, God called me to help refine a proven mechanism that would compel sidelined Christians to return to the Church and become dedicated followers of Christ. While reading a daily devotional, the words describing the original church just jumped off the page at me. The revelation was like a bolt of lightning.

I had been searching for meaning in my life, trying to figure out a way to give back…a way to connect with God. I was struck by the passage depicting early Christians meeting in homes, and I became determined to find a way to make that model work to get sidelined Christians like myself back to the Church.

I had not attended a church for nearly thirty years when I received this revelation. I had never written a book nor participated in a Bible study, but somehow God chose me to be a vessel for this calling. Others before me have laid the groundwork for the revival of this unique church format. My responsibility is to fan the embers of the fires that these pioneers ignited and to bring more clarity to the process of starting a micro-church.

I can state with utmost confidence that my personal contributions to this book were minimal. Over a period of several months, God began revealing His plan to me. Pages and pages of notes lead to a detailed outline. That outline resulted in the book that you are reading. I give all praise and glory to God for this work and thank Him for the calling that He has placed on my life.

As I look back, God had been preparing me for this calling my entire life. It is absolutely amazing how He works! I pray that this book will inspire you and Christians around the world to reengage with God and get back to the Church.

The person who God used to change my life radically is Andrew Wommack. He is truly blessed with the gift of breaking the Word down into understandable language. The revelations that he has received from God are amazing.

I would encourage you to connect with his ministry at awmi.net. He will open your eyes to the truths of the Bible. Andrew Wommack's book, <u>Sharper Than a Two-Edged Sword,</u> is a synopsis of many of his teachings. I am sure it will be as much of a blessing to you as it was to me.

Whether you join the micro-church revolution or connect with a traditional church, now is the time to reestablish a full-time relationship with the Body of Christ. Take a leap of faith today. **Get back to the Church!** I promise that God will bless you.

Additional Resources

Starting a micro-church is an exciting process that can appear challenging at first glance. This book presents the concepts needed to start a church. Additional resources have been developed to guide the micro-church builder through the startup process.

For access to the many tools that will make this inspiring process straightforward, please visit our Micro-Church Revolution website (www.micro-churchrevolution.com).

There are references throughout this book to the specific tools, including checklists, templates, worksheets, plans, and tip sheets. The first tool is the following:

TOOL 1: Micro-Church Startup Checklist—*Provides a detailed listing of the steps needed to start and grow a micro-church and track progress.*

A complete list of available tools is provided in the Appendix. All the tools are included in **Micro-Church Tool Box 2.0** and can be accessed by visiting our website at www.micro-churchrevolution.com.

The reader is encouraged to take advantage of these additional resources that are designed to save valuable time and ensure that new micro-churches are successful in accomplishing God's plan for their church.

May God bless you as you move forward on this journey.

CHAPTER 1

Christianity Today

"Be sober, be vigilant; because your adversary the devil, as a roaring lion, walketh about, seeking whom he may devour." (1 Peter 5:8 KJV)

War on Christianity

Today's Christians are living in extremely turbulent times. Whether believers realize it or not, the Body of Christ is at war. Followers around the world continue to be slaughtered for their faith in Christ. Governments have been focused on eroding the religious rights of Christians for nearly 2,000 years.

Atheists, hell-bent on destroying the Church, are working from within the power structure to discredit Christianity. Funded by wealthy modern-day devils, the enemy is making tremendous inroads into the Christian life. Most believers are ill-equipped for the warfare that is taking place all around them.

Ungodliness rules our society. Evil is prevalent everywhere one looks. Television and movies continue to astound Christian viewers with immoral content. Godless influential people are brainwashing young adults into accepting all of the degeneracy being promoted by special interest groups. Even some churches have strayed so far from God's Word that they could be considered cults.

Society is collapsing around us. Neighborhoods are crumbling with increasing crime, homelessness, and corruption. Morality has fallen so far that it is hard to believe the course can be reversed. This decline cannot continue to manifest without a profound effect on the Body of Christ.

The scene is set for a disaster of biblical proportions, leaving some to wonder if these are the end times. Power shifts around the world create an environment of uncertainty and fear. Radical Islam has generated utter chaos as nations react to diabolical terrorist acts. Mentally unstable, homemade terrorists continue to vent their rage on innocent victims.

Christian symbols are being attacked and removed from public spaces. Separation of Church and State is becoming separation of Church from country. This is enough to alarm even the most ardent followers of Christ who are truly walking in faith and trusting in His protection.

Struggles Within

The American Church has seen better times. Nearly 75% of the population claim to be Christian, yet only 25% of these believers practice their faith on a regular basis. Many of these practitioners actually do not even attend church.

The large percentage of the nation's Christians practicing their faith outside of the traditional church are disconnected from the Body of Christ. These followers may simply pray and read the Bible at home. Many attend Bible studies with other disengaged Christians. Some help others by volunteering with non-profit organizations.

Followers are leaving traditional churches in alarming numbers. It is predicted that by 2025 traditional church membership will be cut in half. It will become much harder for the Church to recover from this downturn as attendance plummets. The United States will become a post-Christian nation if this decline continues to accelerate.

One reason for this deterioration is that millennials are not engaging with the Church as previous generations have. Many traditional churches do not offer what the younger generation is looking for. The worship experience lacks the dynamic environment that today's young adults have in other areas of their life.

Church membership is aging without the participation of this vital age group. Only 15% of young Christians are attending church regularly. The longer this trend continues, the more alienated young adults will become, and the less relevant the Church will be.

A new and exciting church experience is needed to inspire millennials and Christians of all ages to reengage with the Body of Christ. Church participation will continue to decline without a catalyst to turn the momentum around. The micro-church is uniquely positioned to fill this need and to lead believers back into the fold.

State of the Church

The majority of Christian churches in the United States are in a state of stagnation or decline. Growth is being seen in small and very large churches, but the vast majority of churches are in trouble. Only 15% of traditional churches are considered to be in good or excellent financial health. Over 4,000 churches close their doors each year, and only 1,000 are launched to fill the gap.

More than 335,000 Christian churches dot the landscape of the United States. Congregation sizes range from under 100 to over 40,000 persons. Worldwide there are 37 million churches, over 2 billion Christians, and 34,000 denominations. This landscape does not make it easy to present the united front that will be needed to turn the tide on church decline.

The commitment of time and money to support a traditional church typically rests with only 20-25% of the congregation. These key contributors are becoming disenchanted and burning out because of the demands being placed on them. Volunteers are getting harder to recruit. Church culture is changing faster than ever before.

To make things worse, many church teachings and doctrines are not based on the Word of God. Some have twisted what the

Bible says to back up their misguided beliefs. Churches are using invalid Old Testament legalism and a performance-based mentality to stifle members. It is very easy to see how churches can stray from the Word of God and how church members can lose faith in the leadership.

Millions of Christians do not attend church on a regular basis. Some are "CEOs" who show up on Christmas and Easter only. Others have given up on the Church altogether. Who are these sidelined Christians?

Some are church volunteers who gave years of service to the Church only to be discarded because of politics or personalities. Most of these disenchanted members are torn about leaving the Church. They are embedded in a community that they truly love. Some avoid leaving for years until so much damage is done that they are forced to cut ties. This frustrating experience often results in members vowing never to return to the Church.

Many Christians have fallen away from the Church as a result of life's circumstances. Some have not attended services since childhood. Others have committed themselves to Christ but never followed up with their walk of faith with Him. The further down the road they get, the less likely it is that reengagement will occur.

Getting sidelined Christians into the battle will be a challenge. The Body of Christ must take action to get the Church moving forward again. Every follower needs to discover the purpose for which God created them and get about their anointed duties.

Moving Forward

Immediate changes need to be made in traditional churches to stem the flow of refugees. A reengineering of this valid church model will help to compel dissatisfied Christians to stay and commit. The micro-church will act as a mechanism to keep committed Christians engaged as traditional churches inevitably reinvent themselves.

Reengaging sidelined Christians is essential to the survival of our Christian nation. God's Word and a revitalized Church will provide the ammunition needed to fight the war being waged against Christianity. All Christians need to be a part of the great revolution and revival ahead.

One cannot help but believe that God is not pleased with the current state of the Church. Yet His love continues to be poured out on those who believe. His blessings are as real today as they were over 6,000 years ago.

Get off the sidelines and back in the battle. Jesus gives us the same invitation today that He gave to His disciples, "Follow Me." Act on this request now without hesitation.

"These things I have spoken unto you, that in me ye might have peace. In the world ye shall have tribulation: but be of good cheer; I have overcome the world." (John 16:33 KJV)

CHAPTER 2

The Micro-Church

"For where two or three are gathered together in My name, there am I in the midst of them." *(Matthew 18:20 KJV)*

New Testament Church

The original Church was formed nearly 2,000 years ago as Christians gathered in homes to hear the amazing news about Christ's resurrection. The disciples moved from home to home teaching believers and converting unbelievers. The Holy Spirit which came upon them at Pentecost allowed the disciples to perform signs and wonders. These miracles drew crowds and brought thousands to Christ.

Many of these micro-churches during this period operated under the radar to avoid detection by the Roman Empire. Considering the time period, the small church model was extremely effective at spreading the Gospel. This unique forum was used exclusively up until the 4th century A.D. when formal churches started to be erected.

The micro-church has been known by many names since the original churches were formed. The list includes house church, small church, simple church, and organic church. These titles all describe a similar small church model, which has existed in one form or another since Christianity began. This simple format remains a remarkably viable church structure that is growing in popularity around the world.

21st Century Landscape

The modern house church movement that started in the 1960s has morphed into an eclectic mix of church formats. Groups have developed hundreds of models using the house church moniker to carry out God's plan to unite and expand the Body of Christ. Many of these formats would be considered true micro-churches, while some would be better classified as cell churches or planting movements.

No matter what the model or motivation, it is clear that God is moving in this arena and making huge inroads into Satan's well-established kingdom here on earth. Church planting movements that are a part of the micro-church scene in China and other nations are seeking to lead as many people as possible to Christ. These movements are making a tremendous difference in the countries in which they operate. However, they are a far cry from a 12-member micro-church in San Diego, California, that has an assorted network of partners that support a mission serving homeless veterans.

Micro-churches are so diversified today that it is hard to explain exactly what one is, let alone how to start one. This book presents a missional model that seems appropriate to fit the micro-church environment in the United States and other Western nations. The model works extremely well for unchurched Christians who are seeking to reconnect with the Body of Christ and to make a difference.

As much as 10% of the Christian adult population in the United States currently attend micro-churches. The estimated 50% decline in traditional church attendance by 2025 may result in as many as 35% of the nation's Christians taking advantage of this more intimate and dynamic micro-church format in the near future. This huge shift in church platforms will have a profound effect on the Body of Christ.

The return to Christianity's roots is reenergizing believers who have left the Church but who continue to seek fulfillment of God's calling in their lives. Many are finding their purpose after being stifled for years. Others are discovering for the first time the unlimited extent of God's love and grace.

Common Features

The modern day micro-church is unique in that each church establishes a model that fits the specific people that God has brought together and the mission that He is calling them to undertake. The size of the micro-church is a determining factor for many of the common characteristics that these small communities share.

Some of the features that micro-churches have in common include:

- **Small Membership Size**—Most micro-churches consist of 6 to 20 members. The twelve-member church appears to be optimal for facilitating close relationships.
- **Casual Venue**—Members worship in private homes or public places. The casual surroundings allow followers to develop close, sacred relationships.
- **Completely Mobile**—The venue can easily change from meeting to meeting because of the simplicity of this extraordinary church format.
- **Minimal Infrastructure**—The small church requires minimal or no infrastructure with which to carry out operations. A stealth environment allows the church to operate freely in carrying out God's agenda.
- **Bible-Centered**—The church service is centered around Bible study that is based directly on God's Word. Members accept the Bible as the true, authentic, and sufficient Word of God.
- **Non-Denominational**—Doctrines and religious traditions are abandoned for direct interaction with the Word. This allows members to start with a clean slate and to develop a shared belief system.
- **Streamlined Format**—With no infrastructure to maintain or programs to run, the modest community is able to focus efforts and resources on helping others.

- **Efficient Resource Management**—The efficient footprint within which the church is designed optimizes resource requirements, allowing members to achieve more with less.
- **Nominal Legal Basis**—Most churches have no formal organization, legal basis, or financial structure. They are able to operate legally under the radar where resources can be advantageously used for the mission.
- **Kingdom-Oriented**—The micro-church is connected to the Body of Christ through mutually-beneficial relationships that help unite Christians.
- **Expandable Model**—Size constraints make it inevitable that new churches will need to be planted to accommodate membership growth. Churches can be easily replicated because of their unique design.
- **Fully-Networked**—Micro-churches network with other micro-churches, traditional churches, ministries, non-profits, and for-profit businesses for maximum impact.

Size does have an effect on the way in which micro-churches are designed. When designed properly, they are pound for pound more productive than their traditional church counterparts. The focused approach creates a sense of urgency that dedicated members respond to whole-heartedly.

Community Characteristics

The micro-church is built around a sacred community of like-minded followers of Christ. A God-centered mentality allows members to find their purpose and contribute to God's plan for the church to help others. Members thrive in an intimate environment where they are inspired to produce great works that further the Kingdom of God.

Micro-church communities typically share the following characteristics:

- **Intimate Environment**—The community facilitates the social connection that imparts a sense of belonging. Member growth and maturity in Christ are accelerated by this intimate environment.
- **Open Communication**—Open communication eliminates many of the trust issues experienced in other types of churches. The intimate environment rapidly builds trust among members.
- **Shared Leadership**—Micro-churches are controlled by their members through shared leadership. They act autonomously within the Body of Christ, having derived their authority directly from Christ.
- **All-Volunteer**—Members share responsibility for the planned objectives of the church and mission. Each person steps up in their area of expertise to share knowledge and experience.
- **Committed Members**—All members are totally invested in the church and mission. The small membership size compels members to participate fully in accomplishing the shared objectives.
- **Value-Oriented**—Core values are developed firsthand from biblical teachings. These values unite the members and drive them to achieve the calling that God has placed on the church.
- **Divine Purpose**—Churches are established for the express purpose of contributing to God's overall plan. Members truly understand God's love and grace and strive fully to discover and carry out His calling.
- **Vision-Driven**—Activities carried out by the church are vision-driven. Goals and objectives inject a sense of urgency into the church's intent to achieve God's plan.
- **Spirit-Guided**—The Holy Spirit facilitates a direct connection with God, which empowers members to stand confidently in Christ.

- **Like Demographics**—Members with shared demographic characteristics are able to focus on common objectives for advancing the Kingdom of God.
- **Discipleship-Oriented**—Jesus calls all Christians to follow Him and become disciples. The ultimate goal of the micro-church is to spread the Good News, either directly or by facilitating an indirect mechanism that does.

Small Group Dynamic

The small group dynamic at work within the micro-church results in a non-judgmental setting where shortcomings are accepted. A team mentality is instilled in a relatively short period of time as the group melds into a cohesive community.

Community members are generous with their time, money, and other contributions. The selfless group has genuine concern for each member and the people who are served by their mission. This caring attitude allows micro-churches to perform exceptionally as a team while members work together to help others.

Members share many other aspects of life together. A weekly meal commemorating the Last Supper is the focal point of the community. A close family-like bond is developed through participation in the church and mission, as well as other outside activities.

Mission Features

The mission to which a micro-church is called allows members to share the love that God has freely given to them. The ultimate goal of Christians is to pass on what God gives them to help others. The missional micro-church model includes common features that assist members with this pursuit. These features include:

- **Purpose-Driven**—Members of micro-churches are driven to help others. Each church has a purpose that includes directly or indirectly helping those less fortunate.

- **Narrow Focus**—Missions typically serve a small segment of the community and focus on specific services.
- **Fast-Moving**—Accommodating design parameters enables the mission to move quickly and to change directions with little negative impact on momentum.
- **Efficient Operations**—Mission activities are typically designed for economic efficiency. This allows most churches to operate with minimal resources.
- **Impactful Objectives**—Missions deliver maximum relative impact with minimum organizational structure.
- **Well-Coordinated**—The organized approach empowers members to utilize fully their strengths to achieve the objectives.

Most missions are based in the neighborhoods within which the members live and worship. Each mission is unique, typically serving a small segment of the community. Mission activities are integrated with the efforts of outside partners, such as other micro-churches, traditional churches, or non-profits.

Some micro-churches function as a volunteer force that helps to accomplish the mission objectives of another organization. Others join forces with other micro-churches to achieve a common mission. Many simply provide a service that does not require extensive funding or infrastructure.

Micro-church builders should strive to establish consistency wherever possible. This will not only provide uniformity within the overall movement but will make the processes of planting new churches and networking with other organizations much easier. The cohesion created by this consistency will help to bring the Body of Christ into unity.

TOOL 2: Common Feature Worksheet—*Identifies key features that can be incorporated into new micro-churches being designed.*

CHAPTER 3

Sure Foundation

"According to the grace of God which is given unto me, as a wise masterbuilder, I have laid the foundation, and another buildeth thereon. But let every man take heed how he buildeth thereupon." (1 Corinthians 3:10 KJV)

Providing Clarity

Builders use a blueprint to illustrate exactly what needs to be done to construct a building. Micro-church builders need to have the same clarity when planning a church. Christ has already laid the foundation of the Church, which is His Word. Church builders need to use the inspiration of the Holy Spirit gained through interaction with the Word to build upon this foundation.

Many groups have tried to start a micro-church without planning or forethought. A few have been somewhat successful in launching churches using this technique. However, the odds of producing a fruitful church and mission are greatly diminished without the framework of formal planning.

Disorganized churches can languish for years achieving much less than their structured counterparts. Some such startups lead to ultimate failure and a bewildered membership. Other groups do not discover God's calling for the church and thus never truly prosper.

Key Advantages

The micro-church is an exceptional mechanism that has compelled millions of people to establish or renew their faith in Christ. This special way of worshiping helps to accommodate Christians with varying church backgrounds and experiences. Key advantages of the micro-church include:

- **Easy to Start**—Micro-churches can be designed and launched quickly. They are often created in stages that build upon each other.
- **Minimal Cost**—Churches can be operated with little or no capital. Missions are designed around available resources.
- **Efficient Mechanism**—Missions utilize God's resources to the greatest extent possible. The simplicity of the approach makes the mission extremely cost-effective.
- **Manageable Size**—The limited membership size forces the focus to be on commonality rather than diversity. Demographics are easily controlled, allowing members with like interests to achieve common objectives.
- **Customizable Design**—The church is built around the unique knowledge and talents of the group. The mission is designed with member interests and passions in mind.
- **Exciting Focus**—The excitement that comes from being a part of something that is transforming the world instills accountability in members and encourages full participation.
- **Complete Transparency**—The church is run with complete transparency, which alleviates concerns oftentimes experienced with larger churches. The very design of the micro-church leaves no room for concealment. All members are intimately involved with every aspect of the church and mission.
- **All-Inclusive**—The community is able to cater to persons who do not fit the traditional Church mold. Even those who have sworn never to return to the Church can find the micro-church environment intriguing.

No two micro-churches are alike despite the common features that they share. Each church is designed with a unique membership and mission in mind. There are no set rules other than the guidelines that are provided in the Bible. The more tailored the approach, the greater the chances of success. There is no set path, but the objective is the same--building the Kingdom of God.

Key Challenges

Issues can have a greater impact on the low-profile micro-church than on traditional churches, where these issues can hide beneath the surface for years. Problems are typically revealed immediately in the micro-environment and thereby dealt with quickly. The dynamic at work in this small church allows members to be more focused and to react quickly to deal with issues as they arise.

Some of the challenges that micro-churches can encounter include:

- **Economy of Scale**—The micro-church lacks the economy of scale that larger churches experience. Nonetheless, the limited capacity with regard to the church mission is easily overcome by joining forces with other organizations. Sharing a common mission can produce much greater efficiencies.
- **Minimal Infrastructure**—There is typically no infrastructure that can be used for celebrations and events, such as weddings, funerals, and baptisms, that draw families and friends from outside the church. Networking with traditional churches or other organizations that have excess capacity can easily provide the solution to this dilemma.
- **Lack of Urgency**—An unstructured environment does not promote a sense of urgency to execute God's agenda. Churches created without sufficient structure generally encounter growth issues and achieve much less than their organized counterparts. This dilemma can be overcome

through proper planning and design of the church and the complete commitment of the members.
- **Low Tech**—Most micro-churches do not offer the professional worship experience that many traditional churches have. The multi-media extravaganzas presented by mega churches are not practical in the micro-environment. The time and energy saved by not offering this production component can be channeled into achieving objectives.
- **Isolation**—Isolation is clearly not what God intended for the original "micro-church" and should not be the intent of new churches being launched. Connecting with the Body of Christ is essential in achieving the common objectives shared by all churches. These divine objectives are designed to bring the Body of Christ together in unity.
- **Disconnection**—Micro-churches operating without the advantages of networking often end up straying from or limiting God's plan for the church. Achievements are typically minimal and members are under-motivated when operating alone, without the driving force that networking can create. Networking can create efficiencies that are beneficial to the micro-church and partner organizations.

Church Design

Taking the time to anticipate some of the common roadblocks facing micro-churches can mean the difference between success and failure. The upfront effort spent on design work will help the church to build a robust platform from which the start-up church can be successfully launched.

Flexibility is the key to a productive church. Defining a model too strictly will unnecessarily constrain the ability of the church to react to a changing world. The platform should allow for maximum latitude as the church evolves.

Growth is inevitable if churches are following God's plan. Expansion needs to be anticipated and planned for. A micro-church should constantly be making adjustments to accommodate this growth. Regularly planting new churches, adding network partners, and growing the mission are processes that should be integrated into the church model.

There is no set model for the modern-day micro-church. No one blueprint will work for every church. Each new church is different because its members and mission are unique. Examining existing models as a starting point will help in discovering the optimal format for a new church.

Written Plan

A written plan is crucial for communicating the vision of the church to members and partners. The micro-church plan is similar to a business plan. It is used to ensure that all aspects of the start-up process are addressed and that the church and mission continue to thrive into the future.

The plan brings together all the components needed to build a successful church, including a simple reproducible strategy for expanding and networking. It is a living document that will change over time, as the church grows and institutes minor course corrections or major changes to planned objectives.

A church plan is also an evaluation tool that can be used to regularly review progress to ensure that the results are meeting expectations. The plan helps to ensure that the proper objectives are set and that goals are being met.

TOOL 3: Micro-Church Plan Template—*Presents the key components of micro-church design and summarizes the information obtained from the related worksheets.*

Who Should Start a Micro-Church?

Many Christians will be called to start churches as this revolution takes hold. Any follower can be a candidate for starting a micro-church. Some of the likely groups of people that will spearhead this transformation of the Church include:

- Believers who have left the traditional Church and are hoping to get back to the Christian community and a direct relationship with God.
- Families desiring a close, intimate community where they can worship with other families who are in the same life stage.
- Young adults who want to make a difference without the institutional constraints of the traditional church.
- Older adults who want a closer relationship with God and a mechanism to implement His plan in their lives.

Not everyone has the drive and determination that it takes to lead a micro-church startup operation. Banding together with other believers who do have these skills is the first step to overcoming this obstacle. Carefully select others who can offer this expertise to join the journey.

Learning how to discover God's plan for starting a church will be discussed in Chapter 6. Let God take control of the process. Finding the real course of action that He has planned for each and every person should be the goal.

The decision to start a micro-church should not be based on the animosity that a person has towards the traditional Church. Some people who have picked up this book have had serious issues with the Church and do not want anything to do with organized religion. Coming to grips with any underlying issues and being at peace with the Body of Christ before moving on are essential in preventing this resentment from carrying over into the micro-church setting.

"And be ye kind one to another, tenderhearted, forgiving one another, even as God for Christ's sake hath forgiven you."
(Ephesians 4:32 KJV)

CHAPTER 4

Revolutionary Instrument

"Now I beseech you, brethren, by the name of our Lord Jesus Christ, that ye all speak the same thing, and that there be no divisions among you; but that ye be perfectly joined together in the same mind and in the same judgment." (1 Corinthians 1:10 KJV)

Evolution

Micro-churches around the world are as different as the languages and cultures that they represent. One is a part of a massive underground church-planting movement in China. Another is a six-member church in the United States that raises funding for a worldwide ministry. This form of church refuses to be defined, yet it continues to evolve into a movement that will play a key role in the transformation of the Christian Church as we know it.

There appears to be no accurate understanding of where the micro-church stands today as far as the depth and breadth of the movement. This may be attributed to the very nature of this small church format. It is difficult to quantify a movement that is constantly evolving. The fact that many micro-churches remain underground does not help to bring clarity to the issue of quantification.

The lack of cohesiveness within the movement may be a major advantage of the revolution as it moves ahead. There are so many fronts for the enemy to attack that by the time one is engaged, a new one presents itself. Couple that with the worldwide appeal of this church model, and it becomes clear why God is moving in this arena.

The underlying concepts characterizing this small church format are shared by most organizations being defined as micro-

The Micro-Church Revolution

churches. This will be the key to this unique church format being a major player in uniting the Body of Christ during the revolution.

God wants to take micro-churches to the next level. Each modern-day micro-church can have the same impact as the original house churches formed nearly 2,000 years ago. In fact, each micro-church can have an infinitely greater impact, if the potential represented by this unique church model is fully realized.

"Verily, verily, I say unto you, He that believeth on me, the works that I do shall he do also; and greater works than these shall he do; because I go unto my Father." (John 14:12 KJV)

Unification

There have been several attempts to organize the micro-church movement itself. Some effective networks have been formed in the United States and around the world. Yet there have been no real connections made to unite the Body of Christ in its entirety. The revolution will be at full force when these connections start to be made.

Unity of faith can only be achieved when all Christians are of the same mind. The prime focus of the Church must be to achieve this solidarity before Christ returns. The real power of God will be revealed when micro-churches connect with traditional churches, Christian businesses, non-profits, and ministries, and this unity starts to manifest.

It seems impossible for all Christian churches to be of the same mind. Unity will happen if churches focus on the Word of God as it is written. The revolution will help to weed out misguided doctrines, misinterpreted beliefs, and religious traditions that exist in abundance. The micro-church will set the example by centering on Bible-based truths.

Revolutionary Instrument

A consensus of faith will fuel the revolution and help to accelerate the move of God that will transform our lives. The transformation starts with Christians connecting with other Christians. Micro-churches are pioneering this unity of faith by demonstrating that this proven church model remains valid.

"Only let your conversation be as it becometh the gospel of Christ: that whether I come and see you, or else be absent, I may hear of your affairs, that ye stand fast in one spirit, with one mind striving together for the faith of the gospel." (Philippians 1:27 KJV)

Revolutionary Model

The micro-church was certainly a revolutionary model when it was first used to spread the most significant news ever communicated. The message is the same, the model is the same, but the capabilities have increased exponentially.

Today's micro-churches have the opportunity to rival the accomplishments of the most spiritually-connected group of people that the world has ever seen…the disciples. The potential is mind-boggling when considering the millions of Christians who have joined this revolution.

It is important that the effort put forward by micro-churches meet some minimal criteria. Uniformity is required for the micro-church to integrate fully with the Christian community. This consistency will help to create the framework upon which relationships can be built between the various components of the Body of Christ.

The concepts that every micro-church should adopt include basic features that are critical to a unified approach. Each church should be:

- **Bible-Based**—The micro-church must be based upon the Word of God in its purest sense. Doctrines, religious

traditions, and misguided interpretations of the Bible must be kept out of the micro-church environment.
- **God-Connected**—God wants a close relationship with each and every person. Taking the steps to make this connection on a personal as well as church level is important. His blessings cannot be delivered if this communication is not taking place.
- **Service-Oriented**—God envisions fully-functional churches when looking at the micro-church model. Loving and helping others should be the main focus. Integrating a formal mission into the church plan ensures that these vital functions are carried out.
- **Discipleship-Driven**—Presenting salvation to unbelievers is the number one calling of any Christian. The micro-church needs to create disciples who can then go out and present the Gospel. Discipleship should be integrated into every activity of the church.
- **Connection-Making**—God wants the Body of Christ to come together in unity. The more connections that can be made between micro-churches, traditional churches, ministries, Christian businesses, non-profits, and individuals, the faster this unification will manifest.

Micro-churches should make sure that these features are built into each church being started. Meeting these minimal standards will ensure that the church has the structure necessary to carry out God's plan for uniting the Body of Christ.

CHAPTER 5
Full Commitment

"I am the way, the truth, and the life: no man cometh unto the Father, but by me." (John 14:6 KJV)

Going All-In

Micro-churches cannot be effective without the power of God operating through them. Church members must be fully committed to Christ in order for this power to manifest. A direct connection with God needs to be established through the Holy Spirit before embarking on the amazing journey of starting a micro-church.

A full commitment to God involves complete surrender to Him. This "all-in" move is required for God to be able to work through believers to achieve His plan. Each person considering starting a micro-church must tap into this supernatural power, which brings with it the blessings needed to make the church a success.

Commitment

Many people reading this book have committed their lives to Christ but did not follow through with their original promise to follow Him. Others have never taken this important life-changing step. Whatever the situation, it is time to go "all in". Take this opportunity to make a full commitment before moving forward with launching a church.

People who previously accepted Christ as their Savior but did not continue their walk with Him need to fully recommit their lives to Him. God has a plan for each and every one of us. Each person needs to reconnect with Him so that they can discover the calling He has placed on their lives. Make this renewed commitment now using the next section in this book as your guide.

Those who have not accepted Jesus Christ as their personal Savior or are not sure if they did need to make this vital commitment today. It is essential that this simple process be completed before receiving eternal life through Christ. Don't wait another day. It is the best decision anyone will ever make. Skip down to the section below which explains exactly how God's amazing love and grace can be received.

Recommitting to Christ

"Let your conversation be without covetousness; and be content with such things as ye have: for he hath said, I will never leave thee, nor forsake thee." (Hebrews 13:5 KJV)

Commitment to Christ requires follow-through. Many Christians have accepted Christ as their Savior but have a distant relationship with Him. For some people (including myself), this commitment may have come when they were young, and their understanding of what it means to serve Christ was incomplete. For many, the promise to follow through with this commitment has faded over the years to where some may not be sure that they were ever truly saved.

Life circumstances may have prevented believers from discovering the truly blessed life that Jesus has waiting for them. Jesus stands ready to welcome each and every person back to a full relationship with Him no matter what the situation. He will never force a person to make this decision. It is up to each individual to make the move. I encourage every person in this situation to recommit themselves to Him now.

The process is simple. It is much like the initial commitment to Him. The follow-up is the important part. Start by praying the following prayer out loud:

Heavenly Father,

I want to know your Son in all His fullness and glory like I have never known before. Forgive me for failing to follow through with my commitment to walk with Him.

Jesus, forgive me for not giving you full control of my life. Please help me to become the person You want me to be. Teach me how to live a life that will please You. Fill me with Your love and peace that surpasses all understanding. Help me to renew my faith and restore my hope in You.

I acknowledge that You are the true and living God and affirm that Your Word is true. Fill me fully with Your Holy Spirit. Renew my mind so that I may know what Your will for my life is. I dedicate my life to You and commit to following You for the rest of my life.

In Jesus' name I pray,

Amen.

Follow-Through

"But the fruit of the Spirit is love, joy, peace, longsuffering, gentleness, goodness, faith, meekness, temperance: against such there is no law." (Galatians 5:22-23 KJV)

Congratulations on your renewed commitment to Christ. I pray that a renewed walk with Him will bring the fruit of the Spirit and the many blessings that God has to offer. God bless you. Skip down to the bottom of this chapter for some helpful hints about following through with this commitment.

Accepting Christ as Your Savior

The process of accepting Christ as your Savior is simple. The following truths will help bring perspective to the decision that you are about to make.

"For God so loved the world, that he gave his only begotten Son, that whosoever believeth in him should not perish, but have everlasting life." (John 3:16 KJV)

The Father

God existed in the form of the Trinity (Father, Son, and Holy Spirit) before the earth was formed over 6,000 years ago. He spoke and, from His words, the earth and everything in it were formed. Sin entered the world when Adam ate from the fruit of the tree of knowledge in the garden of Eden.

God sent His Son to the earth to institute a new covenant, a covenant where Christ's sacrifice would atone for our sins and God's grace and love would be fully realized. The love that God has for us is inconceivable. God exists as pure and absolute love. Love is the very essence of His being. Lives are changed dramatically when this love is tapped into.

God has loved each and every one of us since before the beginning of time. Before we were born He loved us. He offers this love to all who will believe. He is eager for everyone to accept His Son as their personal savior so that He can reveal this love to them.

"And the Word was made flesh, and dwelt among us, (and we beheld his glory, the glory as of the only begotten of the Father,) full of grace and truth." (John 1:14 KJV)

The Son

Jesus was born into this world of the virgin Mary. He lived on earth for approximately 33 years and never committed a sin. It was not until he was 30 years old that He was baptized in water by John the Baptist and then received the baptism of the Holy Spirit. He then began His short ministry. His death and resurrection was the most profound event the world has ever experienced or ever will.

Jesus was persecuted during His entire three-year ministry, despite the fact that He performed every miracle, sign, and wonder imaginable. His impact was so great that nearly 2,000 years later people still seek Him. There is no doubt of His existence as a result of the impact He made and continues to make in the lives of believers.

The Holy Bible is living proof of Christ's existence as it guides Christians through their daily lives. It remains the most read book in the world because the words are alive and bring true knowledge to believers.

Some people believe that Jesus was just a mere prophet, but He is so much more than that! He died so that all our sins (past, present, and future) would be forgiven. He took all the sins of the world upon Himself on the cross. His suffering was more than it is possible to conceive.

"But the Comforter, which is the Holy Ghost, whom the Father will send in my name, he shall teach you all things, and bring all things to your remembrance, whatsoever I have said unto you." (John 14:26 KJV)

The Holy Spirit

God's grace has already provided everything needed for salvation. All a person has to do is believe and receive Christ into their life. Once we receive Jesus as our Savior, he takes it from there. He activates the Holy Spirit who is already inside each one of us. The Spirit is the one who connects us to Jesus and God. The Holy Spirit is the mentor who will guide each person through this amazing adventure.

Jesus promises that whatever we ask of Him, he will provide. Jesus said, *"And whatsoever ye shall ask in my name, that will I do, that the Father may be glorified in the Son. If ye shall ask any thing in my name, I will do it." (John 14:13-14 KJV)*

God will seek to get these blessings into our lives once faith has been established and we are seeking Him. Believing and having faith are necessary for receiving these gifts. Start by working with the Holy Spirit to remove barriers that prevent these blessings from being received.

Purpose

We were put on earth to serve God. Each and every one of us was created for a specific purpose. He reveals our purpose as we mature in Christ. A believer will desire only to serve Him in this capacity once they discover what their purpose is.

One purpose that we all have is to become disciples of Christ. It is our responsibility to tell others about God's grace so that they too can make the decision to follow Him. God never forces us to do anything. He gave us free will when He gave us authority in the earthly realm.

Jesus is working through us to bring God's plan to fruition. God seeks to unify the entire Body of Christ, so that we will be ready to carry out His will in the spiritual realm when Jesus returns.

The Decision

The Father is the only living God. All others have come and gone. He can start doing miraculous things in a believer's life as soon as they have accepted His Son as their Savior. All we have to do is believe that Jesus died for our sins and that He arose and is now seated at the right hand of God in the heavenly realm.

God's Word promises: *"That if thou shalt confess with thy mouth the Lord Jesus, and shalt believe in thine heart that God hath raised him from the dead, thou shalt be saved. For with the heart man believeth unto righteousness; and with the mouth confession is made unto salvation… For whosoever shall call upon the name of the Lord shall be saved." (Romans 10:9–10,13 KJV)*

Full Commitment

This is the most important decision that a person will ever make so it should not be taken lightly. Those not ready to receive this gift should not rush into the decision. God wants believers to freely accept His Son as their Savior. Be prepared to live a changed life (an inspired life) once this decision has been made.

Leap of Faith

It is as simple as it has been explained. All that is needed is to believe in Him and declare that He has risen from the dead. I pray that you will take this leap of faith right now.

Eternal life is the reward for believing in Him. When Jesus returns we will receive a glorified body that is flawless. We will have no grief, sorrow, pain, or loneliness. But wait!!! If we accept Christ before He returns, we can have all of this here on earth…well, everything except the glorified body.

Please do not hesitate to accept this invitation from Christ. Start learning about the absolute love that God has for each and every one of us. Pray this prayer out loud and believe what Christ has done for you:

Heavenly Father,

Thank you for loving me. Thank you for sending Your Son Jesus Christ to die for me on the cross. I believe that He died for my sins, and I ask You to forgive me of the sins I have committed.

I accept Jesus as my Lord and personal Savior and commit to following Him and Your Word. I believe that He arose from the dead and is seated with You right now in heaven. I look forward to walking with Him and discovering the many blessings that His Word offers me.

Thank you for providing my salvation. In Jesus' name I pray,

Amen.

Transformation

"Therefore if any man be in Christ, he is a new creature: old things are passed away; behold, all things are become new." (2 Corinthians 5:17 KJV)

His Word instantly comes alive in a believer's Spirit the very moment they commit themselves to Jesus. They become a brand-new person. Their life is completely changed at the spiritual level.

For some people, this change will be dramatic. Most will wonder if they were saved because they do not feel any different. Believe in Him and you are saved. It is a decision that I guarantee you will not regret. Follow Christ and He will show you the way.

It is up to each person to take the next steps of faith and begin their walk with Jesus. The objective should be to be more like Jesus every day. Imitating Him is the best path to spiritual maturity.

Here are some helpful tips on following through with this commitment:

- Speak to God regularly in prayer.
- Praise Him constantly for His many blessings.
- Read and study the Bible daily.
- Meditate on His Word and receive revelations.
- Practice being like Christ.
- Emulate His love as an example to everyone you meet.
- Turn away from sin when it comes into your life.
- Seek out other Christians for fellowship.
- Find the purpose for which God has put you on the earth.
- Move forward everyday with fulfilling this purpose.
- Tell others about your commitment and help them find Jesus.

Full Commitment

- Join a church or help to start a micro-church.

Congratulations! May God bless you as you start this journey. Have faith in Him and you will set yourself up for supernatural blessings.

CHAPTER 6

God's Master Plan

"Wherefore the rather, brethren, give diligence to make your calling and election sure: for if ye do these things, ye shall never fall: For so an entrance shall be ministered unto you abundantly into the everlasting kingdom of our Lord and Saviour Jesus Christ." (2 Peter 1:10-11)

Discovery Process

Are you being called to start a micro-church? Is it your idea or God's plan? Have you received a revelation from God confirming your path? Who is God calling the church to help? These are just a few of the questions that need to be answered as part of the discovery process that takes place prior to launching a church.

A person cannot solely rely on carnal rationale in making the decision to form a micro-church. Much of the decision-making process needs to take place within the spiritual realm. Discovering what God has planned is essential when launching a church. Take the time to uncover His plans before moving forward.

Starting a micro-church without spiritual guidance can ultimately lead to failure. God's blessing is what powers every successful church. Seek to have this blessing working within the church being considered. Continue to pursue the Holy Spirit's guidance until convinced through a revelation from God that the micro-church is the answer.

Viable Options

All viable options should be identified and analyzed when seeking God's guidance. Is there another church structure that would better fit the need? Is there an existing micro-church that can be joined? Is there a traditional church out there that might be a better option? Will a traditional church small group meet the need?

Answering these and other questions first will help to eliminate any nonviable options. This will also make it clear as to what options to seek God's guidance on. Present the findings to God and wait for a revelation to be delivered. Once assured that the micro-church is the most viable option, move forward with the remaining discovery process.

Completing this due diligence up front can save many hours of wasted time when inevitable issues arise and the church is forced to back up and start over again. A false start or a complete failure can do more harm than good. Eliminate the potential for this happening by methodically building a micro-church one step at a time with the Holy Spirit leading the way.

TOOL 4: Discovery Checklist—*Presents the steps necessary to perform the initial discovery process.*

God's Plan

Many Christians are not fully aware that God has devised a complete and utterly brilliant system within which the Body of Christ is operating. The goal is to have all Christians "*...come in the unity of the faith, and of the knowledge of the Son of God*" *(Ephesians 4:13 KJV).* Being aligned with this system is essential for every church.

God's plan thus far has spanned over 6,000 years. Many believe that the current Age of Grace is coming to an end. There are just too many prophecies that are being fulfilled for believers not to take this prediction seriously. This makes it even more important that Christians discover their calling and strive to achieve the unity of faith that Christ is bringing about around the world.

The five-fold ministry is the foundational principle of the Church. *"And he gave some, apostles; and some, prophets; and some, evangelists; and some, pastors and teachers; For the perfecting of the saints, for the work of the ministry, for the edifying of the Body of Christ." (Ephesians 4:11-12 KJV)*

God calls some people to the five ministries: apostle, prophet, evangelist, pastor, or teacher. The majority of us are called to support these five ministries. This calling can include anything from being a part of the praise and worship team at a church to being an entrepreneur and making millions of dollars that can be used to support the Kingdom.

Before He even created the earth, God predetermined what each person's gifts would be and the roles that they would play. Each one of us has been assigned to one of these ministries. It is up to us to connect with the Holy Spirit, receive our assignment, and carry out our duties. Utilizing God's power and blessings is essential for a successful micro-church start-up.

A multitude of spiritual knowledge can be tapped into by reading and studying the Bible. It reveals prophetic insight and provides the means by which believers can discover what their part in God's master plan is.

Churches need to build upon the foundation that has been provided by the Bible. The micro-church is modeled after the fundamental structure of the Church, as it is described in the New Testament. Staying true to this proven model helps to ensure success.

Holy Spirit

The Holy Spirit was instrumental in getting each reader to pick up this book. This did not occur by happenstance. The Spirit guides Christians through life. Believers need to be open to receive this guidance and to put it to work in their lives. The "fruit of the Spirit" is available to all those who do.

The Spirit is the connection to the spiritual world that needs to be tapped in order to provide knowledge and guidance to the micro-church. Welcoming the Holy Spirit into the church during the startup process is essential. The Spirit will need to be leading the way if a micro-church is going to thrive.

Putting the Holy Spirit to work within the micro-church is about individual members connecting to the spiritual world and praying that the Spirit will work through each member to unite their efforts. Make this the first step of the process.

Core Members

Don't act alone when making the decision to launch a micro-church. Identify key persons who will help start the church and ask them to participate in this process. The core members are people within the initiator's circle of influence who can form the nucleus of the church and act as the startup team as the church is being formed. Seeking spiritual guidance by engaging like-minded Christians as core members will help to authenticate the revelations received and build upon the knowledge base of the group.

Each potential core member should be evaluated to ensure they are a good fit for the church. Compatible personalities are a must. Core member backgrounds should be examined to discover what complementary skills can be brought to the new church. Select core members who will commit to the task at hand and are interested in becoming members.

Share the vision for the church and mission with the selected core members and enlist their help and input. Schedule a series of meetings to start the process. Meet as a group to share ideas, pray, and study the Bible. Encourage each member individually to seek further guidance from God.

Self-Assessment

As part of the discovery process, a quick self-assessment is in order to determine if the start-up team has the leadership abilities to form the church. The person or team taking the first steps in creating a micro-church should exhibit certain qualities or traits. These traits will help to move the church forward until other members can join the effort and fill in the many gaps that will be revealed as the church grows.

The process is much the same as starting a business. The conceptual stage is very important for laying the foundation of the business. Failure to plan and foresee future obstacles can be devastating to a business. This is why a large percentage of small business start-ups fail within the first year, and the odds are even worse after five years.

Be able to answer the following questions:

- What is the motivating factor for starting a micro-church?
- Is the startup team being called by God?
- Do they have the time and commitment level to follow through?
- Are the minimal resources needed to start the church available?
- Does the start-up team have the personality, tenacity, and leadership ability?
- If not, is there anyone who does possess these traits and can join the effort?

Have answers to these questions before proceeding further with the formation of the church. This book will help the startup team through this important process and allow them to determine if a micro-church is the answer to the questions being asked.

TOOL 5: Startup Team Assessment Worksheet—*Evaluates the strengths and weaknesses of the team and identifies any major obstacles they may face when starting the church.*

Interim Bible Study

Many micro-church startup groups form strategically-focused Bible studies to help discover God's plan for the church. Bible study is an important part of the micro-church worship service. This fellowship and study can help to jumpstart the due diligence process and set the agenda for the impending church.

Center the Bible study around discovering what God has planned for the group. Use this time to grow in Christ and actively wait for an answer from God. Pray as a group as well as individually that He will guide the study. Individual Bible study and meditation on the Scriptures will reinforce this effort.

The group can begin brainstorming ideas for the micro-church and mission during this time period. Many of the processes mentioned throughout this book can also be planned or actually started by the founding members as they wait to discover God's plan. Make this Bible study a launching pad that will propel the church forward when it is finally set in motion.

Spiritual Guidance

Seeking spiritual guidance not only helps validate the calling to start the micro-church but should be used on an ongoing basis to ensure the church stays on the right path. During the discovery period, the startup team should also be seeking God's guidance as to whom the church is being called to help with the mission. The following processes will help to guide the members through the spiritual side of the equation:

Process 1: Prayer

"And all things, whatsoever ye shall ask in prayer, believing, ye shall receive." (Matthew 21:22 KJV)

The process of seeking spiritual guidance starts with prayer. A one-on-one conversation with God needs to be started. This open communication should be continued until an answer is received.

This may seem awkward for some Christians, but God loves this type of interaction through the Holy Spirit. The more that a person is in-tune with God on a spiritual level, the faster His plan will be revealed. Keep the conversations going and the senses focused to receive revelations.

Spending time in group prayer with the core members will help to unify the individual efforts being undertaken. This will also ensure that everyone is asking God for the same thing. Group prayer should be a part of the pre-startup meetings. Participants should be encouraged to follow up with individual prayer and keep the group informed as revelations are received.

Process 2: Bible Study

"For the word of God is quick, and powerful, and sharper than any two-edged sword, piercing even to the dividing asunder of soul and spirit, and of the joints and marrow, and is a discerner of the thoughts and intents of the heart." (Hebrews 4:12 KJV)

God speaks indirectly to people in many ways. Delivering revelations through Scripture is one of His favorites. Take advantage of this powerful tool that God has given us. Reading the Bible and in-depth study of the Scriptures should be daily habits for all Christians. For best results, get into the Word and never stop reading it.

Group Bible study will help to reveal further revelations or confirm those that have been received. Parts of the revelation being received may come from different people. It may require assembling these parts of the puzzle to reveal the ultimate revelation. The interim Bible study described above is a great way to focus on the task at hand, which is determining whether God is calling the group to start a micro-church.

Process 3: Meditation

"This book of the law shall not depart out of thy mouth; but thou shalt meditate therein day and night, that thou mayest observe to do according to all that is written therein: for then thou shalt make thy way prosperous, and then thou shalt have good success." (Joshua 1:8 KJV)

Meditating on the Scriptures being studied will help to facilitate revelations from God. Keeping the Scriptures and the micro-church in mind while silently sitting or going about daily duties will bring understanding and revelation. This is a learned process that will take practice to be able to concentrate and stay centered on the Scriptures. In a short period of time, meditation will become more natural and God's voice will be heard.

Make time daily for meditation in a quiet place. *"Be still and know that I am God..."(Psalms 46:10 KJV).* Meditation can take place at any time, but it is best accomplished in a tranquil environment. Thought can be guided through the process to prevent the mind from wandering. Be still and open to receiving God's guidance.

Process 4: Imagination

"That the God of our Lord Jesus Christ, the Father of glory, may give unto you the spirit of wisdom and revelation in the knowledge of him: The eyes of your understanding being enlightened; that ye may know what is the hope of his calling, and what the riches of the glory of his inheritance in the saints."(Ephesians 1:17-18)

Imagination is a powerful tool for connecting with God. It goes hand in hand with meditation by allowing the practitioner to visualize something in a meditative state. Every aspect of the church and mission can be imagined. The Holy Spirit will guide a person's imagination, and revelations will be received.

Learn to use this tool by disconnecting from this world and plugging into the spiritual world. Maintain a positive attitude, be humble, and cast all cares upon the Lord. Imagine the possibility of starting a micro-church and all of the great works that can be achieved through Christ.

Process 5: Dreams and Visions

"And it shall come to pass afterward, that I will pour out my spirit upon all flesh; and your sons and your daughters shall prophesy, your old men shall dream dreams, your young men shall see visions." (Joel 2:28 KJV)

Dreams or visions can be used by God to deliver revelations. These come to a person directly through the Holy Spirit. The more tuned-in to the Spirit a person is, the more likelihood that dreams or visions will be used to deliver revelations.

Asking God to send a dream or vision can facilitate the process, but there is little more one can do to receive one. Many dreams or visions may need to be interpreted before their meaning is revealed. God is in control on this one, just as He is with everything else.

Revelation Delivery

"And Jesus answered and said unto him, Blessed art thou, Simon Barjona: for flesh and blood hath not revealed it unto thee, but my Father which is in heaven." (Matthew 16:17 KJV)

Spiritual guidance can come in many forms as has been demonstrated above. Sometimes it is a series of small revelations that, when combined, reveal God's plan. Other times they come with a bang, and there is no mistaking that a revelation has been received. Revelations are typically delivered indirectly through the Holy Spirit.

How does a person know if an answer to the question of whether a micro-church should be started has been received? Most revelations are fairly recognizable by the recipient if they are seeking them. Listening and being open to receiving communication from God is the key. Ask God to reveal His plan and then wait for the answer.

The bottom line should be what a person's conscience or spirit is telling them. Do the members have peace of mind about the decision? Does the decision line up with God's will and His Word?

The startup team should also have some idea as to what the church mission will involve before moving forward. The church will be formed around the mission. Knowing who the church is called to help will bring the mission to the forefront where God can use it to carry out His plan.

Allow sufficient time for God's plan to be revealed. Be patient and stay tuned-in to God. Maybe He will lead the group in another direction. The absence of an answer may also be an answer. Continue to wait on God if there is any feeling of apprehension.

"Rest in the LORD, and wait patiently for him." (Psalms 37:7 KJV)

Most people reading this book have been lead to do so by the Holy Spirit. It should just be a matter of confirmation of this unction, through the processes described above, that is needed. God will provide peace of mind about moving forward with starting a micro-church.

Be ready to take a leap of faith once convinced through the revelation being sought that the micro-church is the answer. Submit to Christ, and the Holy Spirit will show how to build the church one step at a time. One should be very comfortable with making the decision to move to the next step in the process. If there is any doubt, wait until God reveals the path through further revelations.

TOOL 6: Spiritual Guidance Worksheet— *Identifies the methods used to seek spiritual guidance and ways in which revelations are received.*

CHAPTER 7

Divine Purpose

"Before I formed thee in the belly I knew thee; and before thou camest forth out of the womb I sanctified thee, and I ordained thee a prophet unto the nations." (Jeremiah 1:5 KJV)

Purpose

The discovery of a calling eludes most Christians, despite the fact that their divine purpose existed before the beginning of time. Many believers die without ever knowing that God had a plan for their lives. The micro-church helps members discover this calling and brings it to the forefront, so that each person can fulfill their predetermined destiny.

The reason a micro-church exists is to fulfill God's agenda for the Body of Christ. Purpose is the driving force behind His plan for each and every believer to help build His Kingdom. This purpose embodies the calling that God has placed on the micro-church and the individual callings that members have on their lives.

God has provided the core purpose under which the Body of Christ operates. The objective is to bring all believers into a unity of faith and maturity in Christ, as they love one another and serve others. Each micro-church redefines these overarching goals to produce a unique purpose that complements God's plan.

Serving Others

The mission is the service element of the micro-church that assists members in accomplishing the calling to serve others. Missions are designed to incorporate God's overall plan into the specific calling that the church will undertake.

The discovery process detailed in Chapter 6 will help to reveal the ultimate purpose of each micro-church. This guiding force will anchor the church to the Kingdom of God so that the church does not get off course. The purpose states what the church will accomplish over the long term to help people.

Establishing the purpose as early in the startup process as possible will avoid confusion and wasted energy. Each micro-church should devote the time necessary to pinpoint the purpose of the church. This purpose is the foundation upon which the church will be built. It will help to define the direction of the church and set expectations for achievement.

It is important that all members are aligned with the objectives described in the purpose statement. Members should also be clear as to how this purpose will be achieved. Each person should be able to fulfill their unique calling directly or indirectly through the church or mission.

Delve into what really drives the members and how they can be motivated. Establish a mission that the members can be passionate about. Integrate the individual callings that members have on their lives into the mission strategy. Members thrive when they are able to contribute their most developed skills to serving others.

Factors

There are many factors that should be considered when defining purpose. A major consideration is the resources required to support the church and carry out the mission. These are the people, assets, and capital needed to accomplish the planned objectives. Identify and determine the potential sources of these resources before finalizing the purpose statement.

A church founded on unrealistic expectations will encounter challenges and potential failure. God usually works in stages that build upon each other. Define a purpose that can be accomplished with existing resources and those that can be expected to realistically be provided by God. The purpose can be expanded later when God provides supernatural blessings.

Don't limit God by understating His calling. Take the time to discover fully what God has planned. Objectives should be challenging for members to achieve. God wants to use every Christian to the best of the abilities that He has provided to them.

The target population that the church will be serving is a key factor when identifying the purpose of the church. Pinpointing this population and determining exactly how they will be served will take time and effort. Zero in on the unique problem that can be solved within the limitations imposed by the micro-church.

TOOL 7: Mission Worksheet—*Defines the mission and the target population that the micro-church will be serving.*

Tailor a solution that will provide the best return for the effort and resources that will be committed. An inefficient mission tends to confuse the participants and erodes achievement. Too much confusion will work against the church to a point where the purpose is lost in the turmoil.

Discipleship is the number one purpose to which Christ calls Christians. It is always assumed that the goal of leading the people being helped to Christ is the primary focus. The ultimate gift is salvation. Establishing faith in Christ will allow the recipient to work out the issues that are preventing them from leading a totally blessed life.

Purpose Statement

The purpose statement is an inspirational affirmation that identifies what the church wants to achieve over the long term to help others. A clear purpose statement is necessary to keep church members and partners inspired, focused, and moving forward. The statement is a powerful motivator that describes the philosophy or driving force behind the church and mission.

Every significant action undertaken by the church will ultimately be contributing to the achievement of this purpose. It is based on the best possible outcome or even stretches beyond what is believed to be possible. The church will be performing this function for the foreseeable future or until the purpose evolves into something larger.

A simple purpose statement might read: "To mature in Christ and grow in unity as a community, while we serve and disciple the elderly within our retirement community; to provide physical and spiritual resources and services that allow the people we serve to age in their homes and live inspired holy lives."

It is worth the effort to identify completely the direction of the church and make the purpose statement a useful tool. Ensure that the statement truly defines the purpose of the church and acts as a motivational tool that can be continually used to guide the membership. Thoroughly planning the overall path of the church and mission will help to achieve more and prevent mistakes that require backtracking and waste time.

TOOL 8: Purpose Statement Worksheet—*Creates an inspiring purpose statement that defines the calling of the church and its members.*

Setting goals and objectives based on the purpose statement is an important process that should not be overlooked. These tools will help define what needs to be done in order to achieve the purpose of the church. They are vital for providing direction and ensuring that the church continually moves forward.

TOOL 9: Goal Summary List & TOOL 10: Goal Worksheet—*Help to define and track goals and objectives in all areas of micro-church development.*

CHAPTER 8
Core Beliefs

"Jesus saith unto him, Thomas, because thou hast seen me, thou hast believed: blessed are they that have not seen, and yet have believed." (John 20:29 KJV)

Statement of Faith

Organizations use core values as the guiding principles that dictate behavior and actions. These values help to distinguish between right and wrong and whether the organization is on the path to fulfilling the planned objectives.

The statement of faith acts as the core values for the micro-church and its mission. These truths are adopted by all members as the guiding beliefs of the church. All actions undertaken by the church are filtered through these Bible-based beliefs.

The statement is a living document that expands as the church receives further understanding through interactions with Scripture and the Holy Spirit. Members are able to stand confidently on these truths. They are beliefs upon which members will never waiver.

It is important to note that this statement is not an attempt to establish a church doctrine. Doctrines throughout history have distorted biblical truths. Some of these misguided principles are to a huge extent responsible for what has gone wrong with the Church today. Religious traditions have handcuffed Christians and are holding them hostage by preventing them from fulfilling God's plan for their lives.

Belief Baseline

The micro-church is an independent group of like-minded individuals who typically come from different walks of life. Many members are predisposed to certain ideologies that have been ingrained in them since childhood. Exposure to church doctrine may have established deep-seated beliefs that are not Bible-based.

Many half-truths have been used to misrepresent the original intent of the Scriptures. These misguided beliefs can be hard to identify and change. Abandoning them is essential in establishing a Bible-based statement of faith that all church members can accept and follow.

Starting a micro-church with a clean slate allows members to develop shared core values. By resetting the baseline, a belief system can be created through direct interaction with the Word and revelations received from God.

There are many controversial subjects currently being debated within the Body of Christ that should be considered for inclusion in the statement of faith. Legalism, spiritual gifts, baptism of the Holy Spirit, and God's sovereignty are just a few of the topics that have divided the Church.

Making a stand in these disputed areas based on biblical truths will help to define the calling of the micro-church and eliminate any confusion that members may have. Don't limit the church by staying away from subjects that are open to question. Aggressively define a biblical platform on which church members can stand and grow.

It is very easy to get off-track when establishing common beliefs. Members can be confident in their stance if each belief is fully vetted through exhaustive Bible study. Avoid taking a couple of words or a verse out of context and basing a belief on it. Verify the facts with related Scriptures on the subject.

Some beliefs need to be ultimately accepted by faith. These are the founding principles of Christianity. The fact that Christ died for our sins and was resurrected is foundational to all other beliefs. This truth is as valid as any has ever been, even though we accept it by faith.

One of the most important beliefs that must be established by every church is the acceptance of the entire Bible as the absolute true Word of God. Making the commitment to stay true to what the Bible teaches in its entirety is essential. This decision is an act of faith rather than a conclusion reached from research. No church can be truly successful without this basic foundational belief.

Belief Defining

A church-specific faith statement should be started as early in the start-up process as possible. This will be an ongoing activity that will take time to fully develop. It is well worth the effort to identify these beliefs so that they can be used as a filter for future decisions.

The belief-defining process starts with a discovery period. In-depth discussions about current beliefs held by the members will help bring out potential issues. This may take some effort to dig deep and identify ingrained beliefs, some of which may be well below the surface.

Start by identifying valid beliefs that members share. Even though these beliefs appear to be authentic, each should be fully researched prior to adding them to the statement of faith. Additional belief subjects can be selected and prioritized for study after vetting these beliefs.

All members need to accept the beliefs that are identified through this process and any further understandings that are gained as the church matures. Try to shoot holes in the validity of each belief by playing "Satan's advocate". The beliefs surviving this process can be added to the statement of faith.

The following are common belief statements that churches have used in statements of faith:

- We believe Jesus died on the cross to pay for our sins.
- We believe that Jesus rose from the dead, ascended into heaven, and will one day return.
- We believe that there is only one true God who exists as three divine persons, the Father, Son, and Holy Spirit.
- We believe that the Bible is the true, authentic and sufficient Word of God.
- We believe that God is the creator and sustainer of all things.
- We believe that all things on earth exist for the glory of God.
- We believe that God has provided everything we have and that we are stewards of His resources.
- We believe that salvation is a free gift from God.
- We believe that the Holy Spirit lives in all Christians who have accepted salvation through Christ.
- We believe that everyone has sinned and fallen short of the glory of God.
- We believe that by God's grace our sins (past, present, and future) have been forgiven.
- We believe that God has given all Christians the power to heal the sick.
- We believe the purpose of our church is to effect discipleship through our mission of serving the less fortunate.

Living Document

The statement of faith is a living document that continues to be refined as the church grows. A periodic review of the statement will be required once the initial beliefs are established. New understandings will be received as the church matures. Adding new beliefs or modifying existing beliefs is an ongoing practice that is a part of the growth process.

Revisiting the core beliefs on a regular basis will not only help to refine the system but will reinforce the beliefs for each member. The final result is a dynamic document that will help to guide the church through any roadblocks that are put before it.

The document should be reviewed by all new members joining the church. A mentor can be assigned to answer questions and further explain each belief. Further teaching may be required for the new member to accept the common beliefs.

TOOL 11: Statement of Faith Worksheet—*Helps microchurch members through the process of creating an inspiring statement of faith.*

CHAPTER 9
Community Formation

"And let us consider one another to provoke unto love and to good works: Not forsaking the assembling of ourselves together, as the manner of some is; but exhorting one another: and so much the more, as ye see the day approaching." (Hebrews 10:24-25 KJV)

Community

What sets the micro-church apart from other church formats is its small footprint that places the focus on the intimate relationships. Micro-churches are able to create unique communities that are molded by God for a specific purpose. The members enjoy close, sacred relationships based on unconditional love.

The micro-community is designed to allow members to thrive in an environment of shared experiences, responsibility, and leadership. The selfless attitude of the members creates a non-judgmental atmosphere where imperfections are accepted and even embraced.

Relationships are based on trust and a desire to help others. Members hold each other to a high accountability standard, which in turn drives performance. The team mentality that is developed helps the small church achieve big wins for Christ relative to the size of the membership.

The community is established around something that is worthwhile because it is part of God's plan. Helping members discover and implement God's vision for their life is a key advantage of the micro-community. Harnessing the unique skills each person possesses allows members to be fully productive and extremely motivated.

God created us to serve Him and each other. He has wired us to desire to belong to a genuine spiritual community. The relationships developed in the micro-church community are supernatural.

Member Engagement

All micro-church members are fully engaged with the church and mission to the extent of their abilities. The main focus of community members is on fulfilling God's plan for their individual lives and for the church. Every person on the face of the earth has something to contribute to His plan. Members are able to discover that calling and pursue it passionately.

Member contributions vary in relation to skill level and abilities. Each member is able to contribute their unique talents to the community. The church uses all of these capabilities to accomplish the planned objectives.

Understanding each member's overall ability to contribute is essential to developing a functional community. Those who cannot afford substantial financial support can offer to provide additional labor or other resources to compensate. Establishing individual contributions up front allows each member to be comfortable with what is expected of them.

Holding members accountable for their commitments is important. Each member is aware of the shortfall that will be created if they do not fulfill their obligations. Contributions may need to be adjusted over time as responsibilities and situations change.

Relationship Building

Community building is an ongoing process that should be a part of the long-term strategy of the church. There are countless ways to facilitate a thriving spiritual community. The church and mission form the nucleus around which the micro-church community is built.

Community Formation

The shared meal is a powerful community-building mechanism that strengthens the bonds between church members. It is a time when members can share aspects of each other's lives and develop the trust that is essential for a fully-functioning community.

Establishing rituals such as the meal connects the members and creates unity. Each interaction brings the members together and further develops the community, whether it is a religious observance, such as Christmas and Easter, or secular celebrations, such as birthdays and holidays.

Taking it one step further by sharing experiences outside of the church setting helps to cement these relationships. Group experiences can range from taking out-of-town trips to forming sports teams that compete in leagues. Any activities that can be shared by two or more members should be encouraged.

Catching a movie, sharing a cup of coffee, shopping, or almost any gathering can be used to build relationships. Outdoor activities, such as golfing, camping, fishing, or hunting, build memories that are not only priceless but strengthen the bonds between members and take the community to a higher level.

The traditional church small group format can also be used in the micro-church to help members grow in Christ while developing relationships. Small groups that undertake parallel Bible studies or explore other biblical teachings help to strengthen the knowledge base of the group and bring members closer.

These small group studies can fill in the blanks that less mature Christians may have. They can also help to provide the fundamentals that all members need to move through the maturity process. Small groups are also a way to fully engage our children, young adults, and others who may not receive the full benefits of the service.

Members develop godly traits as the community develops. These traits are a part of the maturing process, that takes place as the community comes together to learn more about what the Bible has to offer. Identify the traits that the church seeks to develop, and then keep them in the forefront as the members mature in Christ.

TOOL 12: Community Trait Checklist—*Identifies the shared traits that micro-church members will seek to develop over time.*

Safe Haven

A key factor in building a thriving community is providing a safe environment where members feel comfortable and inspired. The trust and love that develop naturally from this backdrop help to produce a secure setting for church members. The informal surroundings of the micro-church permit members to bond quickly.

The small membership size of the church allows new members to assimilate quickly into the community. New members become acclimated to the surroundings and find their place in the group after only one or two gatherings. They are able to start contributing to the church and mission objectives immediately.

Churches should make a concerted effort to address any obstacles that stand in the way of establishing or maintaining this secure setting. Negative elements can be quickly deflected if identified promptly. Paying attention to all aspects of the community environment will help to identify issues.

Team Mentality

Creating a community is similar to team building. Various types of activities can be used to enhance relationships and reinforce roles. The diverse activities that micro-churches promote are designed to instill a team mentality.

The goal of team building is to increase performance. These same principles can be applied to growing a micro-church community. The enhanced relationships achieved through community building allow the church to produce more with fewer resources.

Getting people into the right roles is very important for the growth of the church. An open environment where each person can express their desires and discover God's plan for their life is essential. The church should integrate each person's talents into the game plan to the greatest extent possible.

A second level of fellowship can be established through partners that are closely aligned with the church. Other micro-churches and traditional churches can engage with the activities of the church or mission. The resulting comradery enhances the member experience and builds important ties.

Implicit Trust

Implicit trust is complete trust that is expressed without any doubt. This certainty is achieved by proving one is totally trustworthy through actions that are taken over time. The micro-church community is a great environment for trust to grow. The bonds of the community are strengthened, and Christ-like love is established as initial trust develops into implicit trust.

Reliability and truthfulness are key requirements for developing implicit trust. Micro-church members keep their promises and are not afraid to say "no" when it is called for. A sense of emotional safety is shared by the members, as trust strengthens and true feelings are revealed and accepted.

Any issues related to trust are immediately dealt with. A violation of trust can destroy relationships and send a micro-church into a tailspin. Members should constantly monitor the pulse of the community, so that any trust issues can be mitigated before relationships are affected.

Culture of Giving

One of the main benefits of building a micro-church community is the culture of giving that is fostered. Members are inspired to give their time and resources to the common good that is promoted by the church and its mission.

This sense of sacrifice is first established within the micro-church community as members help each other. A genuine concern for other members is cultivated as relationships develop over time. The spirit of giving is then transmitted to the target population that the mission serves.

Giving comes easier for some people than others. A person's background and resources are the main determinants of a giving attitude. Members need to understand their differences and work towards a culture of giving that encourages unrestrained giving from all members.

Outreach Activities

The recruiting of new members is an ongoing activity for the micro-church community. Most members are driven to the church either through community activities or member discipleship. Finding new members is sometimes less of a problem than attracting too many members to the limited-capacity church. Outreach is typically the solution that resolves both of these issues.

Outreach will be needed to attract new members at various points during the lifetime of the micro-church. The start-up phase is usually one of these times. Outreach can be used to increase the membership level to within the target membership range in a short time.

Planting a new church can help to resolve capacity issues when churches grow beyond their target range. A few church leaders are used to plant the new church. Some of the other members also migrate over to the planted church to help establish it.

Community Formation

Outreach is then used to bring the membership of both churches to within their target ranges.

Church missions oftentimes attempt to achieve maximum results with minimal human resources. Falling below a specific membership level can slow progress or jeopardize the mission. The church can move swiftly to maintain membership equilibrium by creating an outreach plan. This enables them to monitor the membership level and execute the plan prior to the time that it is needed.

Micro-churches can attract new members through indirect discipleship. This natural process produces a gradual influx of new members, which can keep membership levels within range. Members are attracted to the church as a residual effect of the outside relationships being developed by the micro-church community.

Lives can be saved simply through the love that members display for each other. Nonbelievers are searching for this type of love in today's godless society. The natural progression of members emulating Christ and showing kindness to everyone will result in nonbeliever interest in joining the church.

"By this shall all men know that ye are my disciples, if ye have love one to another." (John 13:35 KJV)

Outreach Methods

Micro-churches are limited to the type of outreach methods that can be deployed. General outreach that attracts many people can completely change the membership mix and send the church off in a different direction than that of the established objectives. Outreach needs to be focused on attracting a few additional members who meet the target member demographics.

Some of the methods that can be used to find new members include:

- Discipling by individual members.
- Designing mission activities to include member recruitment.
- Recruiting members who volunteer for mission activities.
- Maintaining a limited social media presence.
- Leaving fliers at key locations.
- Asking for referrals from the many contacts made by the church and mission.
- Interfacing with the neighborhood on a limited basis.
- Involvement with local community activities.

An outreach plan identifies the methods that will be used to recruit new members and the timing with which each method will be deployed. The plan should identify both ongoing activities and those activities to be used on a periodic basis. All of the outreach methods should be developed and in place, so that they can be implemented quickly when needed.

TOOL 13: Member Outreach Plan Template—*Creates an outreach plan that can be quickly executed when member outreach is required.*

Communication

Effective communication is vital for the small micro-church community. Important information needs to be disseminated to members on a regular basis. A breakdown in communication can leave a big gap in expected results. The micro-church is affected to a much greater extent than a larger congregation if one person is left out of the loop.

Determining what types of information will be communicated and how this information is to be broadcast will be determined by church demographics, mission objectives, network structure, and the overall technical proficiency of the members. Establishing the most efficient modes for circulating

Community Formation

information will help to maximize the effectiveness of the church and mission.

Communication efforts should not be such a burden that the cost in time and money outweighs the benefits. Carefully choose the modes, frequency, and content that best utilize resources and facilitate the sharing of information. Selecting one or two members to oversee communications for the group avoids confusion and wasted time.

Remember that micro-churches are not only communicating with members. There are also outside partners and any number of other organizations and individuals that need to be kept in the loop. Finding modes of communication that can serve both internal and external customers is one of the keys to effective communication.

TOOL 14: Communication Worksheet—*Identifies the best modes of communication for the church and mission.*

"Let no corrupt communication proceed out of your mouth, but that which is good to the use of edifying, that it may minister grace unto the hearers." (Ephesians 4:29 KJV)

CHAPTER 10

Disciple Development

"Go ye therefore, and teach all nations, baptizing them in the name of the Father, and of the Son, and of the Holy Ghost: Teaching them to observe all things whatsoever I have commanded you: and, lo, I am with you alway, even unto the end of the world." (Matthew 28:19-20 KJV)

The Great Commission

Matthew 28:19-20 contains the last instructions that Jesus gave to his disciples. The importance of this great commission is magnified by the fact that it was Christ's parting command. Discipleship is without exception one of His highest priorities for every believer. Believers must mature to a point where God can work through them before this command can be effectively carried out.

The micro-church is one of the best platforms for developing disciples. The original house churches were formed for this very purpose. Modern-day micro-churches are compelled to have the same objective in mind. All activities carried out by the church should include a discipleship element.

Spiritual Maturity

The goal of the micro-church is to facilitate the process of spiritual maturity that develops disciples. Few people actually reach the pinnacle of full maturity, which produces agape, or God-like love. Every Christian should strive to master all the qualities it takes to be Christ-like, no matter how elusive this process may be.

There is an infinite wealth of knowledge and wisdom that can be gained by continually seeking maturity in Christ. Spiritual maturity is marked by knowing how to handle problems and to apply biblical principles to every circumstance of life.

The world, the flesh, and Satan all conspire to prevent Christians from applying these principles. Imitating Christ in our daily lives focuses believers on the objective of attaining maturity.

Micro-church members should strive to gain knowledge and understanding in ways that advance their spiritual maturity. The church plays a key role in this process by facilitating the varying maturity levels of its members in such a way that all members benefit from the message being presented. A well-conceived spiritual path helps the church meet this challenge.

Maturity is impossible without the constant guidance of the Holy Spirit. Born-again believers have activated the potential for the Holy Spirit to work in their lives. The micro-church can accommodate the flow of the Holy Spirit through the biblical principles that are practiced.

Maturity Objectives

There are objectives that Christians must meet before attaining agape love or full spiritual maturity. Christ-like qualities are developed as believers work their way through the process. Micro-churches assist their members by providing a structured pathway to maturity and an environment where they can practice these required traits.

The following are some of the Christ-like qualities that are gained along the way:

- Wisdom (James 1:5, James 3:17).
- Moral excellence (2 Peter 1:5, Romans 12:2).
- Patience (2 Peter 3:9, Proverbs 15:18).
- Perseverance (James 1:12, Galatians 6:9).
- Faithfulness (Proverbs 28:20, Luke 16:10-12).
- Humility (James 4:6, 1 Peter 5:6).
- Self-sacrifice (Matthew 6:33, 2 Timothy 2:3-4).
- Self-control (2 Timothy 1:7, Proverbs 25:28).
- Devotion (Luke 16:13, Philippians 4:8-9).

Disciple Development

- Compassion (Ephesians 4:32, Galatians 6:2).
- Love (John 13:34-35, 1 Corinthians 13:4-8,13).

Maturity Process

Spiritual maturity is not something that happens overnight. It is a gradual process that needs to be built into daily Christian life. The maturity process involves understanding God's Word, renewing one's mind, and applying what is learned to help others. This is both a group and individual experience that can be integrated into all micro-church activities.

The process starts with a person accepting Christ and then developing a desire to grow in Him. The key mechanism that facilitates maturity is the Word. Spiritual growth comes from absorbing the Scriptures and meditating on them as much as possible. God then uses the Word to provide revelations through the ministry of the Holy Spirit.

Applying this revelation knowledge is the most important step in the maturity process. The micro-church assists with this process by reinforcing what has been learned and providing mentors for those members who are less spiritually mature. The focus of the church is on accelerating the spiritual growth of those being mentored.

Bible-Centered

Maturing in Christ as a micro-church member requires a commitment to a variety of activities centered around the Bible. Every person seeking maturity needs to read and study the Word on a daily basis. Keeping our minds in the spiritual realm as much as possible reduces exposure to the carnal world and the sin in it.

Bible reading is the process of reading portions of the Bible on a regular basis. Bible study is the in-depth examination of Scriptures using a variety of resources. Daily reading and study expose a person to the Word and open them up to receiving revelations that can be applied to their life. Every micro-church member should commit to these activities.

Members should also commit to meditating on the Word as part of their daily routine. Focusing on a specific passage or even a word or phrase that stands out during the reading or study process will help the Holy Spirit to communicate revelations. Find a quiet place to further contemplate and patiently listen for answers from God.

Prayer is an important part of all Bible study and reading activities. Ask God for guidance and wisdom to interpret, understand, and apply the Scriptures. Pray that further understanding is received as questions arise. Ask the Holy Spirit to provide the answers to the specific questions. Thank God for the revelations that are received through prayer and praise.

Spiritual Path

The spiritual path of the micro-church is the structured plan to move members through the maturity process. It involves designing church teachings and activities around achieving the goal of spiritual maturity. The path is structured to accommodate all members, no matter what level of spiritual knowledge, experience, or maturity they have.

Identifying the individual maturity level of each member will help to set the learning agenda of the church. Studies should be challenging for members at all levels of maturity. Mature members can take the lesson to the next level by studying areas of deeper meaning within the Scriptures. There are always additional revelations that can be squeezed out of each verse.

The spiritual path of the group should be planned with the input of the entire membership. A well-conceived plan minimizes the confusion and increases the knowledge and revelations received. Members should develop a five-year plan

Disciple Development

that provides the framework from which to pursue spiritual maturity.

The spiritual path will need to be adjusted over time as new members join the church. The plan should anticipate changes in the maturity mix that will result as churches are being planted. Some of the more mature members are often called upon to plant the new church. This loss of knowledge and wisdom results in a need to modify the spiritual path to accommodate the maturity level of new members who take their place.

TOOL 15: Spiritual Path Plan Template—*Defines the spiritual path of the church and monitors the progress that is achieved.*

Discipleship

Putting the wisdom and knowledge gained from the process of spiritual maturity to work is the ultimate objective of the micro-church. Leading others to Christ so that they can in turn become disciples is the fulfillment of the great commission.

The micro-church needs a formal discipleship plan that arms members with the tools necessary to disciple unbelievers. This plan should be a prioritized component of the spiritual path so that all members will have the knowledge and experience required to disciple unbelievers effectively.

Each micro-church should build discipleship into every activity that the church or their mission undertakes. The discipleship plan should include the methods that will be used to provide the opportunity for discipleship both at the group level and individually.

TOOL 16: Discipleship Plan Template—*Identifies the opportunities that the micro-church can provide to their members for discipling unbelievers.*

CHAPTER 11

Member Demographics

"*Now ye are the Body of Christ, and members in particular. And God hath set some in the church, first apostles, secondarily prophets, thirdly teachers, after that miracles, then gifts of healings, helps, governments, diversities of tongues.*" *(1 Corinthians 12:27-28 KJV)*

Demographic Characteristics

•Traditional churches commonly have diverse memberships that mirror the population of the surrounding neighborhoods. Members of all age groups and backgrounds come together to worship in this larger church format. The church typically operates an assortment of programs designed to meet the needs of each member.

Micro-churches have limited diversity as a result of the finite size of the membership. The demographic characteristics of the core members tend to establish the overall composition of the group. Identifying the ideal member demographics and recruiting members with these characteristics helps the church to stay focused.

Jesus wants all Christians to be as productive as possible so that every person on earth will have the opportunity to receive salvation. It is each member's responsibility to maximize their contribution to this ultimate cause. The narrowed demographics help to make the micro-church more efficient so that greater success can be achieved.

Few micro-churches actually have members who meet all of the desired demographic characteristics. God will often send unique individuals into the church's path who do not fit the profile for a reason. The positives that these people bring to the group outweigh adherence to a demographic target. Be open to accepting anyone into the group who will help to maximize the effectiveness of the church.

What is important is that all micro-church members need to be on the same page. Too much diversity in some areas such as age group can be detrimental to the overall effectiveness of the church. Identify target demographics that will help to select members who fit the objectives of the church and let God do the rest.

Target Member Profile

Micro-churches should develop a target member profile that describes the ideal member demographic characteristics that best suit the church and mission. Narrowing the field allows the church to recruit persons whose backgrounds correlate with the planned objectives. This profile is used as a guideline when new members are recruited.

The personalities and life experiences of the members should complement each other if a thriving community is to be established. These commonalities are essential for the success of the church. An open-ended profile can lead to long-term issues that can greatly reduce the performance of the church.

Generational or life-stage differences can limit the capabilities of the group. Micro-church members share life together. Like-minded persons in the same life-stage generally have common experiences and can relate more fully to persons of similar backgrounds. The group focus is enhanced when members are looking through the same filter.

Churches profit from diversity at many levels, including ethnicity, education level, and maturity in Christ. Don't limit God's plan by defining a member profile that is too narrow or limiting. Use this tool as a reminder of what characteristics will work best for the church in advancing God's agenda.

Member Demographics

A demographic profile builds a picture of what a typical member would look like. It is an attempt to identify the specific population segment that is being sought to join the church. Some of the characteristics that should be considered when creating a target member profile for a micro-church include age, marital status, education level, employment status, income level, residence location, and availability.

Remember that the demographic profile is a target. Potential members should not be rejected based on the member profile. If the church is truly sanctioned by God, He will send the right people.

TOOL 17: Target Member Profile Worksheet—*Describes the ideal demographic characteristics in identifying new members.*

Target Membership Range

Membership size affects many aspects of a micro-church. A target membership range can be used to help the church work within the limitations of this church model. Having enough members to create a community and achieve a mission, while not exceeding the size constraints of the micro-church, can be challenging.

The venue is one of the key determining factors of church membership size. The maximum capacity of the venue will set the ceiling for attendance. Parking limitations may further limit the size of the church. The church venue should be selected with the anticipated target membership range in mind.

The mission also plays an important role in church size. Having adequate capacity to carry out the mission is essential. A clear understanding of the mission is needed before the target member size can be finalized. Future expansion of the church and mission should also be taken into account.

Most micro-churches have a membership of 6-20 persons. The attendance level will vary over time depending on the growth stage of the church. A range should be established within which the membership will grow and fluctuate. The total range should be large enough so that normal variations do not trigger a need to take action.

Twelve-person churches appear to be the optimal membership target for maintaining close relationships. This level is large enough to develop a viable community but requires minimal infrastructure and other resources.

The twelve-member church may want to use a target range of 6-18 persons. There are no absolute limits on church size. God will provide direction for each church.

TOOL 18: Target Member Range Worksheet—*Sets limitations on membership size based on specific factors affecting the micro-church.*

The top and bottom of the target range represent the points at which an action needs to be taken to achieve equilibrium. On the top end of the range, the action level may signal that planting a new church should be underway. The bottom end of the range may signal that a more aggressive recruitment process needs to be deployed.

Keep in mind that an overcrowded church interferes with the community dynamic. When the venue has reached maximum capacity, the burden becomes overwhelming for the host and logistics become cumbersome. Monitoring the membership level will help to foresee the need for action. Be prepared to take action when it is called for.

CHAPTER 12

Member Contributions

"For as we have many members in one body, and all members have not the same office: So we, being many, are one body in Christ, and every one members one of another." (Romans 12:4-5 KJV)

Tasking

Membership size usually compels each micro-church member to assume responsibility for multiple functions related to the church and mission. Tasking is the process of determining what the specific tasks are, efficiently arranging them into roles, and assigning them to the best person available.

The underlying requirement for micro-church members is that each person be fully engaged to the best of their abilities. A decentralized or shared leadership structure makes it necessary for every member to step up and utilize their skills to the fullest extent possible.

Placing people in the right roles is essential. Members who are assigned the appropriate roles flourish in their position, because they are achieving God's purpose in their lives. Misplacement of members can slow progress, cause major confusion, and stifle success.

The core members of the church set the tone by designing the initial leadership structure around their unique gifts. As the church grows, new members are strategically placed into positions where they can contribute the most. The church may need to recruit new members with unique skills to fill a specific need.

Role assignment is not as easy as finding the best person for the job. God has a plan for each member as well as an overall plan for the church. Both of these pursuits should be considered when placing people into specific roles. Incorporating the calling of each member into the roles being assigned will inspire them to fully engage.

There is typically a constant shifting of responsibility to balance loads and to utilize abilities most efficiently. Some key members will need to be replaced as they leave to plant a new church. Attrition may also necessitate temporary or permanent adjustments. This fluid environment allows each member to continue to refine their desired role.

Consider member availability before making the assignments. Consult each member to determine if they can dedicate the time needed to assume a specific role. Be willing to make adjustments to accommodate member concerns.

TOOL 19: Member Tasking Worksheet—*Places members in the best church and mission roles to take advantage of their skills and interests.*

Leadership Roles

The majority of traditional churches have paid leadership who are responsible for all aspects of the church. These positions make most of the decisions on behalf of the entire congregation and are a dominating factor in determining the direction of the church.

Micro-churches are no different from other churches when it comes to the need for leadership. With no paid positions, the onus is on the members to provide guidance through shared leadership. This decentralized leadership model works quite well within the micro-environment, where there is a ceiling on membership size and manageable mission objectives are pursued.

Micro-churches are designed so that members have leadership roles in areas where their skills can be best utilized. Each member has leadership ability in some area. These skills need to be identified and utilized to the fullest. Determining member strengths, weaknesses, and interests is crucial for placing each person in their proper leadership roles.

Spiritual Leadership

One of the main objectives of the micro-church is to facilitate the spiritual maturity process of its members. The spiritual leader is often the most challenging position for a startup church to fill. There can be a rather long learning curve if a member does not have some formal training or experience. Lack of leadership in this area can reduce the pace of spiritual maturity for church members.

A dedicated spiritual leader helps to keep the maturity process on track and moving forward. Churches that have a member who has a spiritual leadership background and can focus on accelerating the group's maturity process are truly blessed.

Recruiting an experienced or trained spiritual leader to fill this key role is a strategy that can be used by micro-churches. This approach is very worthwhile if the majority of the members are in the early stages of spiritual maturity. Finding the right person who fits the group can be daunting but is worth the effort.

Sometimes borrowing a leader from another church or Bible study group on a temporary basis can help bridge the gap, as church members are developing their skills. The part-time spiritual leader can help to get the church on the path to maturity, until such time that others can step up to take over the role.

Churches should also consider having some members develop leadership skills through formal training. Spiritual leadership skills can also be obtained by attending Bible school or other formal training. Online coursework and other resources can get a member up to speed fairly quickly.

Shared Spiritual Leadership

A micro-church can be successfully formed without an experienced spiritual leader. Shared spiritual leadership can be the answer for many churches where no members have formal training or experience. This leadership format engages multiple if not all of the members in the teaching process. The experience can be very rewarding with the right mix of personalities and maturity levels.

While there is generally a slower maturity rate up front with shared leadership, this option can be an excellent learning experience for the members undertaking this task. It allows more members to participate in the spiritual growth that takes place when preparing to present Scriptures and leading Bible study discussion.

Coordination is the key to group spiritual leadership. Assigning one person as the organizer helps to keep the process on track. Mentoring those who do not have the necessary skills will help to ensure that the opportunity is shared equally and that meaningful knowledge is being shared.

TOOL 20: Spiritual Leadership Worksheet—*Determines how spiritual leadership will be established and what resources will be needed.*

Balancing Loads

Some roles can be very demanding even in the micro-church setting. Consideration should also be given to a plan for rotating these responsibilities. The challenges of difficult positions can cause burnout over time, if a mechanism is not put into place to monitor and makes changes when necessary. Preventing burnout is important for the overall health of the church and mission.

Cross-training of leadership positions can provide the solution to burnout. An ongoing cross-training program should be built into the process. Even if only a portion of the duties of a position are isolated and assisted with, the relief can be enough to prevent burnout. Keep a close watch on morale so that changes can be quickly made.

Some leaders and their skills will need to be transferred when new churches are planted. Constant growth in leadership abilities needs to be built into church activities. Both internal and external training opportunities should be made available on an ongoing basis.

Rotating responsibilities regularly is a good practice even with less demanding positions. Balancing the load is also important. Even though one person may want to take on a larger burden, relying too heavily on any one member can hinder growth and create an unbalanced power structure.

Providing members with the proper resources is important. Evaluate each role and pinpoint those areas where resources can be used to shorten the learning curve and save valuable member time. Identify the tools necessary to make the task easier and more rewarding.

CHAPTER 13

Venue Selection

"And daily in the temple, and in every house, they ceased not to teach and preach Jesus Christ." (Acts 5:42)

Venue Logistics

There are many logistical considerations that need to be addressed when starting a micro-church. Most are related to the unique church venue and the facilities needed to carry out the mission. The absence of a dedicated structure for worshipping presents some challenges that should be evaluated before a micro-church is launched.

The sky is the limit as far as the location of the micro-church venue. The key is to determine whether or not the specific venue can satisfy the needs of the church and meet all of the underlying requirements. Venue requirements for the mission may have to be addressed separately if the activities to be undertaken call for more extensive facilities.

Site Options

The micro-church venue is nearly always an informal setting. The majority of churches use member homes as the worship site. Some meet exclusively in one home while others rotate among several homes. Multiple locations can refresh the worship environment and make the experience more dynamic. Rotating the meeting site also reduces the burden that is placed on a full-time host.

Sharing facilities with other micro-churches, traditional churches, or mission partners should all be considered when searching for a location. The excess capacity of these more formal locations can be tapped with little or no burden being placed on the property owner. Other potential venues include:

- Parks
- Restaurants
- Coffee houses
- Christian bookstores
- Workplaces
- Office meeting rooms
- College dorm rooms
- Study halls
- Malls
- Youth centers
- Libraries.

Venue Analysis

Analyzing venues for potential issues is wise even if there is only one site being considered. The process should include identifying concerns and determining the actions needed to resolve them. Evaluating multiple venues will help to narrow the possible choices and pinpoint the best alternative.

Take all factors into consideration before making a final decision. Ensure that all of the requirements for the specific micro-church are being met. Investigate potential legal constraints that can become barriers. Identify options that can mitigate these limitations.

Constraints from local authorities and homeowner's associations can stifle the micro-church. Home-based business regulations can come into play for certain venues. It is prudent to plan the church around these requirements before they become a roadblock.

The use of some facilities may require that permission be obtained from the property owner or municipality. A permit may be necessary for some public venues. It is always a good idea to get the approval of a business owner before planning to use their property, even when it is a public place.

Business owners usually welcome the patronage of the group but may place some restrictions on the meeting. Establish a relationship with the owner and treat them as a partner. Help to make their business a success by using their products or services as often as possible. Seek out Christian businesses wherever possible.

TOOL 21: Venue Analysis Worksheet—*Evaluates potential venues and selects the best option available to the micro-church.*

Neighborhood Impact

Impacting a neighborhood with traffic, parked cars, and noise is always a concern. Micro-churches are coming under attack in courts of law by persons being impacted by their activities. Evaluate how neighbors will be affected by the church and weigh any negative findings against the value of a particular venue.

Adequate parking is one of the biggest challenges for the micro-church. Some communities have parking restrictions that limit access. Many restricted communities do not have the capacity to accommodate outside vehicles. Consider all possibilities, such as parking offsite and shuttling or carpooling to the venue. Park as many vehicles as possible in the driveway and garage, if a private home is being used.

Keep in mind that the venue is within the area of influence for the church and mission where discipleship efforts will be undertaken. Members should set a good example within the neighborhood. They should be able to be identified as Christians simply by the love that is shared and kindness that is shown to everyone.

- Make a positive impression by informing neighbors of the potential impact. The number one discipleship opportunity for Christians is the people who they come in contact with every day. Exploit these opportunities by establishing relationships with neighbors and showing them the incredible love that God has to offer.

Site Requirements

A quiet atmosphere with minimal interruptions is important for the church service. Members need to be able to hear and concentrate on what is being said. The middle of a busy restaurant does not fit this requirement, but an outdoor corner of a coffee shop may. Members should be conscientious about not impacting others who share a public venue.

Minimize disruptions of the church service by identifying potential issues ahead of time. Disruptions break the flow of the service. They can prevent the members from receiving the full message being presented. Creating a learning environment that optimizes communication is essential.

Pets can be another issue by disrupting the service or making certain people uncomfortable. Everyone has different views on pets. Some may tolerate them out of respect for the host but prefer not to have to deal with them. Pets should be isolated if there is any indication that members are concerned about their presence.

The venue should be clean and free from potential hazards. Tripping and falling issues should be eliminated to the greatest extent possible. Furniture should be comfortable and of adequate quality as to prevent potential injury. The venue should be an environment that is comfortable and inviting.

Air temperature can be a major venue issue. A comfortable temperature is required for members to maintain full attention. The heating and air conditioning systems should maintain an acceptable temperature range when church members are present. Additional equipment such as fans may be needed to resolve temperature or ventilation issues.

Venue Selection

The meeting area within the venue needs to be large enough to accommodate the upper limit of the target membership range. Adequate comfortable seating that is not overly crowded is optimal. Guests should have flat surfaces to set beverages and Bible study materials.

Bathroom facilities must be located in the immediate vicinity. Members should be able to use the facilities quickly and get back to the service. Evaluate the restrooms for cleanliness and adequacy. Many churches will take a break during the service, and multiple persons will need to use the facilities simultaneously.

Most micro-churches share a weekly meal to honor Christ's sacrifice and to build community relationships. This meal is typically scheduled after the service but can be enjoyed at any time. The venue should have adequate food service facilities to accommodate the meal and keep the food heated or cooled to a safe temperature.

Venue Options

Always have at least one backup location to where the service can be quickly transferred. The weather is unpredictable and can cause major issues for some venues. Unforeseen circumstances, such as the illness of the host, may also require a sudden change of location.

Cancelling the service should only be considered when the majority of the members are unable to attend. The church size makes it easy to reschedule the service to another time during the week, if needed. Communicating any changes quickly and accurately is essential.

Reducing the burden of hosting by rotating the venue is always a good idea. Hosting the micro-church service and meal can be very challenging. A lot of time and effort can go into this weekly activity. Breaking down the tasks involved in hosting so that others can assist with this activity also helps to lessen the hardship.

Integrating Children

Children represent challenges and blessings when it comes to the micro-church. Thought should be given as to how children and young adults will be integrated into the service, if the church will be including families in the target demographic. The objective should be to maximize the learning experience for everyone involved.

There are generally three options for accommodating children in a micro-church service. The first is to integrate them fully into the service by starting a family-oriented church. This requires that the children be at an appropriate age and maturity level so that both child and adult are able to learn.

Each situation will be unique. The actions of younger or uncontrollable adolescents can hinder the flow of the service to the extent that the interruptions are too much to expect members to deal with. Evaluate the specific children before making the move to integrate them into the service. Remember that children will grow and mature as time passes. Anticipating this change will help to make sound decisions.

The second option for integrating children is to have a secondary area where they can learn and play under the supervision of an adult. This option accommodates the children better by providing a learning environment that is based on the maturity level of each child. The oversight of this group can be rotated to reduce the impact on any one person.

Micro-churches with teenage family members may want to consider a third option of implanting a church. The implanted church is operated by the young adults under the mentorship of one or more adults. This service can be held at a different time

Venue Selection

and location, so that the mentors can participate in the adult service and devote the time necessary to guide the young adults through the process.

CHAPTER 14
Worship Service Design

"But the hour cometh, and now is, when the true worshippers shall worship the Father in spirit and in truth: for the Father seeketh such to worship him." (John 4:23 KJV)

Worship Service

Micro-church members gather together in an informal setting to worship God. The customizable service format is designed to fit each unique group of believers. Some structure is required for the service to be functional and meaningful. Too much structure tends to work against the simplicity of the intimate micro-church environment.

Most churches avoid modeling the service strictly after the traditional church format which is designed to accommodate the masses. Many of the components of traditional services and Bible studies are used in some form by the micro-church. The way in which these elements are incorporated is what sets the micro-church service apart from other churches.

The micro-church service format will also tend to vary from week to week. Sometimes special features, such as video teachings, special praise and worship, or guest speakers will be included. At other times the entire membership may attend the worship service of a partner church. Services may even be held around a mission event being sponsored by the church.

The sky is the limit as far as how the service will appear, when it is held, and what features are included. Keeping the service exciting as well as enriching allows the micro-church to compete with the multi-media extravaganzas of large traditional churches without the added effort required to stage such events.

Service Elements

The built-in flexibility of the micro-church enables each church to mold the service into a format that fits the unique community. Elements that are in common with traditional churches are often modified to tailor them to the smaller setting. Each church puts its own twist on the service elements to produce an exclusive gathering.

Fellowship typically takes place both before and after the service. Some members arrive early to catch up and to set up for the service or meal. Many churches share a meal after the service that extends the fellowship for hours. Other churches detach the meal from the service making them separate events.

Announcements are made by a designated member at some point in the service. These communiques can deal with a wide variety of subjects. Some of the information that can be conveyed includes news on upcoming events, the theme for next week's meal, or reminders of planned activities. Celebrations, such as birthdays or anniversaries, can be announced during the service and observed during the fellowship that follows.

Mission information can be communicated during the announcement segment but is typically better suited for a separate forum. Some churches may incorporate an informal mission meeting into the day's events. Others may have more formal meetings on another day of the week. The scope of the mission usually dictates the need for and frequency of these meetings.

Contributions will be accepted at some point during the service if formal tithes and offerings are received by the church. Many churches have a basket or box where members can contribute any time before, during, or after the service. Others incorporate a formal offering segment into the service.

Prayer is a key element of the micro-church worship service. Some churches have a prayer minister or ask members to assist with the prayers that are offered during the service. The service typically begins with the opening prayer after all members have been gathered together. A closing prayer brings the service to an end and sums up the wisdom and knowledge received during the service.

Prayer requests can be taken at any time during the service. Time should be set aside to pray as a group for other members, their families, or for any other concerns that members may have. Prayer is a powerful medium through which the needs of the members can be realized. Micro-churches should ensure that this vital activity is used effectively and given a high level of importance.

Time should also be provided to accommodate testimonials from church members who are inspired to present them. Testimonials can be interjected during any part of the service. Setting aside a specific segment of the service for testimonials usually works better for the flow of the service.

TOOL 22: Worship Service Template—*Helps to design the worship service and ensure that key service elements are included.*

The Teaching

The teaching is the most prominent element of the service. The spiritual leader will customarily start the teaching with a summary of the lesson plan, which allows members to focus on the subject. This may include a complete overview of the setting and characters that will be delved into during the teaching.

The reading of Scriptures will take place throughout the service as the lesson unfolds. Sometimes members will be asked to read a portion of the Scriptures being presented. Often the Scriptures are so integrated into the presentation that asking others to read breaks the flow of the message.

The leader presents the message which is typically a condensed version of the traditional sermon. Spiritual leaders present their take on the topic after extensive study and meditation. Conclusions are reached by the leader that are further discussed and debated by the entire group. Sometimes questions may be posed by the leader to help start a dialogue on the subject after the leader has finished.

Open discussion of the teaching is one of the elements that sets the micro-church service apart from traditional churches. Member questions are usually saved until after the leader finishes the presentation. Once the subject is open for discussion, members are able to ask questions, provide other takes on the subject, or bring up related subjects.

The leader wraps up the service at the appropriate time by summarizing what has been learned. The key takeaways may stand on their own or be carried forward for further discussion by the entire membership or in small groups. Follow-up assignments from the day's discussion can be made at this time. The next week's lesson may also be introduced to get members familiar with the next subject and looking forward to the upcoming service.

Micro-churches may present multimedia content during the service as either the main teaching or to reinforce what is being discussed. Some churches will view the readily available sermons or teachings of recognized ministers as part of the service and then expand on the content through discussion.

Chromecast is a great low-cost tool for casting content from a web browser or hand-held device to a television. Media, such as video, live streaming, and audio, can be transferred to the larger television screen for viewing or listening by a group. Documents that are stored online can also be accessed during a service.

Other tools that can be useful during the service include white boards and post-its. Leaders can use the white board to illustrate or take notes as the subject is discussed. Post-its can be used by members to write down questions without interrupting the service. These questions can be placed on a wall or board and discussed after the presentation.

Providing members with the written material prior to the micro-church service allows them to get more out of the lesson being taught. A Bible study plan is very useful for organizing the materials in a structured format. The plan ensures that all elements of the lesson are communicated.

TOOL 23: Bible Study Template—*Organizes the worship service teaching and documents subjects that have been covered.*

Praise and Worship

Praise and worship are an important part of the micro-church service. Some churches are blessed to have members who are musically talented and can perform or lead the group during the service. Others rely on recorded music or music videos for this function.

Some churches downplay praise and worship altogether because of a lack of resources. This is a mistake if it is the case. God loves and deserves for believers to give Him praise and worship Him through music. He is pleased even if the members sing unplugged hymns out of tune.

Churches should establish a body of music that has a wide appeal. Select music that everyone can enjoy and participate in singing. Cycling through the music so that there are different songs each week keeps a fresh perspective that is centered on giving God the praise He is worthy of. The music can also be synced with the teaching to bring more meaning to the service.

Playing background music before and after the service helps to create a praise-filled atmosphere. There are numerous services that make this process easy. Pandora is one of the most popular services that offers both free and pay music options.

Selecting a genre, such as Christian Contemporary, is an easy way to get great background music for free. The user can customize the experience and eliminate the occasional advertisements for a few dollars a month. Keep in mind that this is background music. The sound level should be adjusted so that members can easily carry on a conversation while the music is playing.

Consider designating a member to facilitate the praise and worship portions of the service. Praise leaders should be able to inspire members to join them in honoring God with praise and song. Placing the proper emphasis on praise will encourage members to continue the practice at home and wherever they go.

Worship Schedule

The day and time of the worship service should be established by taking the schedules of each member into account. All members are important to the success of the micro-church where one person is a significant percentage of the congregation. It should be assumed that all members will be attending every service. The size of the church membership usually allows for each member's schedule to be accommodated.

Sunday is typically the day observed by Christians around the world as the day of worship. Organized religion has designated this day even though the Sabbath originally started at sundown Friday and ended at sundown Saturday. The significance of the micro-church service is not lost if it is observed on another day. Jesus promised that He will be with us whenever we gather.

The service schedule may need to be changed periodically to adjust for the time of year or rescheduled at the last minute to compensate for weather. Be open also to making occasional adjustments to better meet needs of the members once the church has settled in. Strive to get full participation by all members.

Most micro-churches meet at least weekly. Activities, such as the mission or outside events, will increase the frequency that members meet or communicate. The mission may take on a dynamic of its own requiring much greater participation. The schedule should allow for all members to be able to participate in church and mission activities.

CHAPTER 15

Important Observances

"For I have received of the Lord that which also I delivered unto you, That the Lord Jesus the same night in which he was betrayed took bread: And when he had given thanks, he broke it, and said, Take, eat: this is my body, which is broken for you: this do in remembrance of me. After the same manner also he took the cup, when he had supped, saying, This cup is the new testament in my blood: this do ye, as oft as ye drink it, in remembrance of me." (1 Corinthians 11:23-25)

Communion

Christians have been sharing Holy Communion for nearly 2,000 years. Communion began on the same night that Jesus was betrayed. He shared the Last Supper with his disciples, breaking bread and sharing wine as a symbol of his impending sacrifice. The very next day Jesus died on the cross for our sins. The significance of this momentous event is not lost by the micro-church community.

The regular observance of Communion serves as a reminder to believers of what Jesus did for them through his death and resurrection. The Bible is not clear as to how often Communion should be observed. Jesus said it should be done often, but he did not indicate how often. The disciples observed Communion daily during the Apostolic era.

Some believe that sharing Communion too often could cause some of the meaning to be lost. The frequency is not as important as the believer's attitude when partaking in Holy Communion. Traditional church observance of Communion ranges from weekly to yearly.

Many micro-churches observe Communion on a monthly or quarterly basis with related teachings that are tied to the theme.

Others conduct a weekly ceremony as part of the service. A few churches have a self-service Communion table that allows members to privately partake of Communion before or after the weekly service.

Some traditional churches limit the people who can conduct a Communion service to ordained members of the clergy. No such restrictions are indicated in the Bible. This would lead most Christians to believe that any person who has been born again can conduct or participate in a Communion service.

Making Communion a part of the micro-church service is important from a biblical and spiritual standpoint. Christ deserves recognition for the sacrifice that He made on the cross. Believers should be reminded daily of the significance of this event. Every church should integrate the observance of Holy Communion into their regular activities as often as practical.

TOOL 24: Communion Service Template—*Assists with the design of the Communion service and the selection of related Scriptures.*

Baptism

There will inevitably be a need for the micro-church to perform baptisms, as members and the people they serve receive salvation. The baptism ceremony admits a person into the Christian community by acknowledging the salvation experience that has already occurred. The commemoration is important because it represents the forgiveness and cleansing from sin that comes from faith in Jesus Christ.

There are several methods of baptism that traditional churches perform. Full immersion is the biblical method that more fully symbolizes the washing away of a person's sins. The person being baptized can be submerged completely under water or can stand in the water while more water is poured over them.

Important Observances

There is no right or wrong way to baptize a person. Symbolism is the most important part of the ceremony.

The baptism ceremony should be reserved for those who are mature enough to recognize the significance of the salvation that has been previously received by them. There is typically a period of preparation for the person being baptized to be able to understand fully the decision that has been made to follow Christ. Allow ample time for the maturity process to begin and for the ceremony to receive the significance that it deserves.

The logistics of performing a baptism can be problematic for some micro-churches that do not have the facilities to perform the ceremony. An ideal location for many churches may be the backyard pool of one of the members. Bodies of water, such as lakes, oceans, or rivers, can be challenging but are certainly options for the micro-church. The best option may be the facilities of a traditional church with which the church has established a partnership.

The Bible does not specifically address the question of who can perform baptisms. It appears from the New Testament that being a disciple of Christ or a good Christian would qualify a person. Most micro-churches will want to rely on the most mature Christians in the church to perform the ceremony. Alternatively, pastors of partner churches could be used for this function.

The underlying objective is for the person being baptized to have a comfortable and rewarding experience. Take the time to determine the best method and venue for the church to perform baptisms. Make the ceremony a special event for the entire church community.

TOOL 25: Baptism Service Template—*Determines how baptisms will be handled and assists with the design of the service.*

Special Events

Events such as weddings and funerals represent a special challenge for the micro-church. These gatherings are traditionally held in churches, but they typically bring together a larger audience than the standard micro-church venue can accommodate. The entire church along with extended family members and friends will participate in these ceremonies.

A great solution to this dilemma is for the micro-church to establish relationships with traditional churches that have the facilities and availability to hold these larger events. Churches should already be creating these connections as part of the networking process which is discussed later. Make sure that partner churches can help to fill this need when making networking decisions.

The celebration of regular events, such as birthdays, anniversaries, and holidays, typically take place within the micro-church venue. Public places can also be used to make these events special and out of the ordinary. Bringing church members together for these types of events helps to build community and bond relationships.

CHAPTER 16

Breaking Bread

"That which we have seen and heard declare we unto you, that ye also may have fellowship with us: and truly our fellowship is with the Father, and with his Son Jesus Christ." (1 John 1:3)

Community Meal

The focal point of the micro-church community is the shared meal that commemorates the Last Supper and Christ's sacrifice. This is a joyous occasion where the entire community comes together typically on a weekly basis. During the meal, relationships are built, trust is established, and love is deepened.

The regularly-shared meal is a trademark of the micro-church community. Making the commitment to share a weekly meal will help to establish the importance of this vital activity. This practice will keep members close and focused on the objectives of the church and mission.

TOOL 26: Meal Planner Template—*Organizes the shared meal and ensures that key elements of meal planning are incorporated.*

Meal Scheduling

Most micro-churches share the meal after the church service. A typical service may start late Sunday morning and the gathering can carry over to the late afternoon with the shared meal immediately following the service. There is no set day or time that the meal can be scheduled. Members should have the time to be able to relax and enjoy fellowship with each other.

Each church will need to identify the best time for the meal that fits their unique membership. Keeping the schedule flexible will help to make the meal a regularly-celebrated practice. Some churches may suspend the shared meal during certain times of the year, such as holidays where members typically spend time with their families.

Be prepared to reschedule the meal around other church activities that may interfere occasionally. When a crisis hits, use the meal as a gathering point to support each other. The meal day and time may also be changed during certain times of the year when weather or daylight hours become an issue.

Meal Logistics

At least one member should be responsible for the organization of the meal. This duty can be rotated periodically or even weekly. If these responsibilities are shared, protocols should be established so that no important tasks are missed when planning and overseeing the meal.

Some churches may prefer that smaller groups be tasked with providing the meal on a rotating basis. This gives the other members a break from the duties of preparing food on a weekly basis. Other churches permanently assign specific tasks to members according to the skills and resources of each person. Some churches may blend these approaches to best meet the needs of the church and the abilities of individual members.

Establishing a theme for each week's meal will keep the meal fun and help members to determine their contribution to the meal. A signup sheet can be provided at each service to help organize the following week's meal.

TOOL 27: Meal Signup Sheet Template—*Organizes each meal and serves as a reminder to the members of their contributions.*

The meal organizer should scan the completed signup sheet and send it out early the following week as a reminder to each member. Without the organization that this and other tools provide, a meal can be a hit-or-miss proposition. Make sure that the meal is properly planned so that the members can fully enjoy the festivities.

A checklist is a great tool for covering all the bases for the meal. It is very helpful if the organizer duties are rotated on a regular basis. The list can include a step-by-step process in sequential order or may just include a listing of materials and important reminders.

Best Dishes

The best food to serve for the micro-church meal are dishes that are easy to make and handle. Most foods should be prepared and cooked ahead of time, if possible. Preparation areas are in high demand when the festivities begin, and the cleanup adds to the burden of the host.

Casseroles have been the king of group meals for many years. Most are easy to make, inexpensive, and can serve a lot of people. The timing of the cooking of the casserole may present some problems. Most dishes should be fully cooked before the service and held at serving temperature.

A close cousin to the casserole dish is the crockpot. The cooking process can be started at home and then finished at the venue when using this handy tool. The crockpot can also be used to keep pre-cooked dishes warm for hours.

Salads are a must for group meals. Typical salads can range from a simple green salad to a seafood pasta salad. It is easy to adjust ingredients of salads to accommodate the theme of the meal. Salads can be both a main dish and a side dish depending on the ingredients used.

TOOL 28: Meal Planning Tip Sheet—*Provides additional tips on planning the micro-church meal.*

Beverage Service

Beverages are usually served during the entire time that the micro-church members are gathered together. Establishing a beverage area will assist with isolating spills and help with the flow of the service and meal. One person should be responsible for overseeing the beverage service and making sure that adequate supplies, such as ice, are replenished.

Hot drinks, such as coffee or tea, are fairly easy to keep available if the machines used have adequate capacity. Many members bring their favorite beverages to share with others. Brewed coffee is usually cheaper to serve than the single-serve option. The size of the group and what they prefer to drink will dictate the best method of serving the beverage.

Water is the most consumed beverage at micro-church gatherings. Many people are not accustomed to drinking water straight from the tap. Even some refrigerator filters leave much to be desired as far as taste. Bottled water is an option but it can present some issues. The bulkiness and weight of water make it difficult to handle. Keeping the water cold can take valuable refrigerator space unless coolers are used.

CHAPTER 17

Legal Framework

"Let every soul be subject unto the higher powers. For there is no power but of God: the powers that be are ordained of God." (Romans 13:1 KJV)

Legal Formation

Most micro-churches are categorized by the IRS as being unincorporated associations. This classification is simply a group of people meeting for a common purpose. Micro-churches fitting this category can receive donations and carry out related activities. They are protected under the U.S. Constitution from government involvement.

The unincorporated association may be the best status for many low-profile micro-churches to maintain. This classification works well, if the activities undertaken by the church produce minimal liability exposure and the mission does not require extensive funding through donations.

Unincorporated association status does have its limitations. The disadvantages of being unincorporated include: States do not formally recognize the existence of the church; members can be liable for the liabilities of the church; the church cannot enter into contracts or agreements; the church is unable to file lawsuits; and the church cannot own or transfer property.

Many micro-churches will find it necessary to open a bank account in order to carry out mission activities. This can be difficult if the church is operating as an unincorporated association. Banks need documentation that a formal organization exists including a tax identification number before an account can be opened.

Creating a formal legal structure may be a better option when micro-churches are called to undertake sizable missions or the liability associated with the church or mission is substantial enough to require mitigation. Members should seek legal advice before making any decisions as to the legal status of the church. There are a number of options that should be explored before making a decision.

TOOL 29: Legal Structure and Liability Worksheet—*Explores legal structures that may make more sense for specific micro-churches and potential areas of liability.*

Incorporation

One of the most common avenues for micro-churches to take is to incorporate as a non-profit. Corporations enjoy many advantages including: they are a legal entity recognized by the state; they can own and transfer property; they can receive a bank loan; they shield members from liability; directors and officers are indemnified; they can enter into contracts and agreements; and they can sue someone who wrongs them.

Donations are tax-deductible for donors when churches obtain 501(c)3 tax-exempt status. Most persons who donate money or other assets to a non-profit expect to be able to receive a tax deduction for their contribution. It is hard for non-profits to attract substantial contributions without official 501(c)3 status. Obtaining this status is a separate process that typically occurs after incorporation.

Some of the disadvantages of being a corporation include: the costs involved with forming the corporation; reporting requirements; record-keeping responsibilities; and the effort needed to draft by-laws. Some of these requirements are minimized because of the size of the micro-church, but the church would still be subject to regulation.

Legal Framework

Of main concern for the micro-church is that the board leadership structure required for incorporation is contrary to the shared leadership model of the church. Board meetings are mandatory and the church is forced to follow the guidance of the board. There are also limitations on how long board members can serve. Thought should be given to how these requirements will be dealt with if the decision is made to incorporate.

The only advice that can be provided is that the micro-church should seek the assistance of professionals, such as lawyers, accountants, and financial advisers, when any decisions of this type are made. The money is well spent knowing that the church is on solid ground with legal decisions that are made. Seek out Christian professionals who can be used in the future as part of the micro-church team.

Evaluating Liability

Liability can come in several forms for the micro-church. Members can be personally liable for the actions of other church members, for injuries (to members, visitors, or recipients), or for the debts of the church. These types of actions are rare but should be considered by the micro-church.

Much of the liability that a church may be exposed to can be mitigated by properly designing the church and mission. Start with an evaluation of the anticipated relationships that will be formed and interactions that will take place with the public. Mission activities and their funding requirements are also areas where concerns can be identified and alleviated.

Play devil's advocate when looking for potential liability. Look at the worst-case scenario in each area and examine how the church and the individual members could be affected. An attorney can provide significant help in this area.

The micro-church should consider incorporation and liability insurance to help cover potential losses where substantial liability exists. Board members and officers can also be insured against personal liability. The best protection against litigation is for members to understand the areas of potential liability and to manage the exposure.

Micro-churches should not have to worry about liability issues. Identifying these issues up front will help to minimize the exposure. The church or mission should be redesigned if there is cause to worry.

Decision Making

The legal structure of the church can affect the way in which decisions are made. The shared leadership is constrained when boards or other legal structure constraints are placed upon the church. The decision-making process may be more challenging when it is shared by the members, but it fits the small group dynamic better.

Many of the major decisions during the startup phase of the micro-church will be made by the core members as a group. The decision-making process changes as the church is launched and other members join. A majority of members should have input into decisions that affect the direction of the church and mission once a church is underway.

Open communication is the key to a healthy micro-church community. A transparent process with an open forum for decision making allows the church to develop trust and grow as a group. It eliminates the resentment that some people may feel when left out of the decision process. It also increases the potential that all viable options are vetted.

Gaining a consensus of members on important decisions in a timely manner can be difficult. Each church will develop its own power structure based on the personalities of the members

Legal Framework

and their responsibilities. The founding core members are presumed to have the last word when major decisions are not supported by all members.

Decisions are made every day that can affect the church and mission. Identifying up front what types of decisions need to be brought to the entire membership is essential. Minor decisions can be delegated to the appropriate individual or group of individuals who have responsibility for a specific function.

Establishing protocols for decision making gives all members a clear understanding of their authority level. It is important to be precise as to who has the authority to make decisions and to what level it extends. Protocols help to validate the choices being made and allow members to move forward with confidence.

Identifying issues as early in the process as possible will help members to focus on solutions before matters inappropriately resolve themselves or increase in severity. Any preemptive measures that can be taken to minimize negative consequences should be identified and acted upon as quickly as possible. The church can then move forward with resolving the issue in an expeditious manner.

TOOL 30: Decision Process Steps—*Presents a typical decision-making process for use by the micro-church.*

Decisions affecting the direction of the church, use of resources, or other significant determinations should be fully vetted. All members should be involved with the decision if there are numerous solutions that can produce varying results. Having the full perspective of the membership allows for more meaningful decisions to be made. Seeking the answer through prayer will help to pinpoint the ultimate plan of action.

TOOL 31: Decision Process Worksheet—*Provides a step-by-step worksheet for making decisions.*

CHAPTER 18

Resource Requirements

"Give, and it shall be given unto you; good measure, pressed down, and shaken together, and running over, shall men give into your bosom. For with the same measure that ye mete withal it shall be measured to you again." (Luke 6:38 KJV)

Activity Support

Micro-churches require some resources no matter how informally the church is designed. Members typically provide the majority of the labor and resources needed for church activities. No formal tithing is typically required to support the church itself. Members supply any need that may arise by sharing the financial responsibility.

The micro-church mission, however, may take on a life of its own. External funding in the form of donations may be required to meet the mission objectives. If these resources are minor, members may be able to gift them to the mission or directly to the recipient. A business structure may need to be formed if more extensive funding is needed.

The optimal mission strategy is for the micro-church to join the established mission of another church or non-profit. This can take the form of directly volunteering for mission events or providing a complimentary service for a niche population that the mission serves. This micro-mission is part of the main mission which undertakes all of the financial obligations associated with the endeavor and manages the liability associated with the venture.

Another viable option is for a group of micro-churches to form a network through which all funding and other resources pass. This option works best when the network consists of closely-tied churches, such as planted churches that have a common mission. One of the churches forms a non-profit with 501(c)3 status and oversees the network as their mission. This church can also provide support activities, such as fundraising for the network.

Resource Needs

The resources needed to launch and sustain a mission will be a key factor in the selection of a mission and its ultimate design. Essential resources may need to be identified and secured before committing to missions requiring heavy outlays of money and other resources. Look for opportunities to reduce the resource requirements of the mission during the planning stages and throughout the lifetime of the mission.

A comprehensive resource analysis should be completed before any serious design work is started on a mission. Know what resources are needed before proceeding. Have reasonable expectation that the required resources are available or attainable within a reasonable time period before attempting to launch a mission.

Most missions can be phased in over time so that resource concerns can be minimized. The church can also start with fundraising activities and delay the launch of the actual mission until adequate funding is generated. There is usually a solution to a funding dilemma that can be built into the mission design.

This may require that partnerships be explored during the design phase of the mission to pinpoint sources of funding or other resources. Donors who can provide direct contributions may need to be identified before moving forward. Obtain pre-commitments from donors to ensure that pledges are secure. Identify backup resources to cover those contributions that do not materialize.

Resource Requirements

Accumulate resources until there is adequate funding to launch the first phase of the mission. Deploy resources in the most economical fashion possible. Remember that these are God's resources for which the micro-church is called to be good stewards.

TOOL 32: Mission Resource Worksheet—*Identifies the resources needed to undertake the micro-church mission and their potential sources.*

Added Capacity

Many micro-churches require more manpower to carry out their missions than their memberships can supply. Non-member volunteers can be used to increase capacity, if the church requires a larger workforce to accomplish their mission objectives effectively. These volunteers can support the church or mission directly, or they can be called upon to participate in specific events where increased capacity is needed.

The power of the volunteer is amazing. God calls people to serve in this support capacity. The lives of both the recipient and volunteer are enriched by the mission. Most volunteers look forward to the next opportunity to help and become loyal to the mission.

The added capacity that volunteers bring to the mission may mean the difference between a micro-church being able to start their own mission and having to use another organization's mission to fulfill their calling. Smaller churches should explore the use of volunteers to increase capacity to where an effective mission can be started.

TOOL 33: Volunteer Utilization Worksheet—*Explores the potential for volunteers being used to expand the scope of the mission.*

Fundraising

Most missions will initially be funded by the members of the micro-church. Attracting outside funding is easier when the mission has a track record. Churches can highlight accomplishments and use the testimonials of the people reached by the mission to help with fundraising.

Consider smaller mission projects that efficiently use the limited resources when first starting out. Ensure that results are well documented so that improvements can be made, if necessary, and the impact of the efforts can be used for attracting additional resources.

Missions with large capital requirements usually depend upon fundraising to finance activities. Unfortunately, fundraising can take precious human resources away from the already challenging mission objectives. Fundraising activities should be designed to get the greatest benefit possible from the resources being expended.

A micro-church needs to develop a fundraising strategy that makes the most efficient use of member time and effort. The strategy should also establish the methods to be used for fundraising activities and the frequency of the events. Identify resources needed to carry out fundraising activities and look for ways to minimize capital requirements.

There are many standard fundraising strategies that can be deployed. The membership size of a micro-church limits these approaches to a handful. Typical funding sources include members, individual donors, business sponsorships, and fundraising events. The strategy should identify creative methods of raising money that fit the specific mission being planned.

Identifying donors or sponsors who can provide money or resources will help to minimize the ongoing fundraising activities of the church. This can be a difficult way for a small church

Resource Requirements

to obtain funding because of the size of the mission. Fundraising events or creating small businesses that fund the mission are more likely paths for the micro-church.

The people and organizations that provide funding or other resources for the micro-church mission should be engaged on an ongoing basis. These relationships need to be cultivated and the donors properly thanked for their contributions. Keeping them well informed of mission activities will compel them to give more in the future.

TOOL 34: Fundraising Strategy Worksheet—*Establishes a strategy for raising the resources needed to fund the mission.*

Giving

Micro-church members should be of the mind that all things have been provided by God. He created the heavens and the earth and everything in them. We are simply stewards of His resources. God expects us to be sowing into His Kingdom so that the Church can be built up and come into a unity of faith.

Members should not construe the fact that there are no formal tithing requirements for micro-churches to mean that tithing is unnecessary. It is clear from Scripture that financial blessings will elude those who do not sow into the Kingdom according to their means.

The micro-church should accommodate the opportunity for members to give in some capacity. Alternatives should be provided by supporting the missions of partner organizations or other ministries, if the church and mission do not require the financial support that depends upon tithing.

Members should be encouraged to give if the need exists within the church. Some members are able to tithe. Others may not be able to give on a consistent basis. What is important is that the law of sowing and reaping is facilitated through the church.

The amount of the gift is not as important as the act of giving. Jesus promises to reward those who give to the Kingdom. The financial blessings are unlimited on His end. Failing to give in some capacity shuts the door for these blessings to be received.

All avenues for giving should be made available to members and donors. These mechanisms for giving can include a basket at the church service, automatic deduction from checking accounts, mail-in envelopes, and acceptance of credit cards.

Transparency

Money and resources utilized by micro-churches should be handled with complete transparency. The misappropriation of funding has been the downfall of many church leaders over the years. Setting up a system to prevent this from occurring at the micro-church level needs to be a priority. Churches should be able to track and account fully for all activities and resources.

Two or three persons should be designated to handle the tithes, offerings, and donations received by the church. This openness ensures that funds are counted accurately and verifies the receipt of the donations. Envelopes should be provided so that cash donations can be tracked.

The church should maintain a ledger that documents all sources of funding and their uses. This can be as simple as a checkbook ledger but should provide as much information about the transactions as possible. More formal accounting techniques will need to be considered for micro-churches that receive substantial donations or that form a legal entity, such as a non-profit organization.

CHAPTER 19

Mission Design

"I have shewed you all things, how that so laboring ye ought to support the weak, and to remember the words of the Lord Jesus, how he said, It is more blessed to give than to receive." (Acts 20:35)

Defining the Mission

There are limitless possibilities available to micro-churches when defining a mission. Taking the time to design a mission that fits God's calling and melds the unique abilities of the members is worth the effort. This sets the church up to receive supernatural blessings that can accelerate achievement of the objectives.

Some of the directions that God has lead micro-churches in include:

- Joining forces with an established mission to enhance or complement their calling.
- Directly discipling unbelievers by inviting them to the church service and regularly planting new churches.
- Distributing Bibles or other literature to local or international ministries.
- Visiting hospital patients, discipling, and praying for healing.
- Assisting veterans and active duty families to meet their needs.
- Starting a business and funneling profits into other missions.
- Developing a micro-church network and assisting new churches to get started.
- Fundraising that supports a missionary or ministry.

- Producing a product that can be sold at a profit to support a mission.
- Planning and hosting Christian-oriented events, conferences, retreats, or training programs.

Researching what other missions are doing will help the micro-church to decide what type of mission to form or join. Evaluating the missions of established organizations, such as churches, non-profits, ministries, and businesses, can be of immense help. Search for missions that are undertaking the same type of activities or are serving the same target population that the church plans to assist.

Identify what these organizations are offering for the specific population the church will be serving. Make note of any ideas that present themselves during the search that can potentially be used by the church to enhance the mission or make it more efficient.

Look for churches and organizations with which potential partnerships can be forged. Make informal contacts with these organizations to learn more about their missions. Begin brainstorming the concepts upon which a unique micro-church mission will be formed.

Delivery Methods

The size constraints of the micro-church make it necessary to design the mission around available resources. Some churches are large enough to take on an in-house mission. Other smaller churches may find it more advantageous to participate in a shared mission or concentrate on specific activities, such as fundraising.

Micro-churches can either directly deliver services to the target population or indirectly provide resources that other organizations use to provide the services. Factors such as membership size and demographic characteristics dictate how the church will help others through mission activities. God will give the church a specific calling, but it is up to the church to determine what specific activities will be undertaken and how they will be delivered.

A direct mission is one that the micro-church initiates and is primarily responsible for. The church works directly with the recipients to deliver the products or services being provided. Mission partners indirectly assist with these activities. Partners can also be closely tied to the management of the mission.

Indirect missions typically provide support for another organization's mission. This can be in the form of supplying a volunteer force, conducting a fundraising effort that produces resources for another mission, or providing a specific product or service that supports a partner.

Producing resources for other churches or organizations can be one of the most efficient mission formats for the small micro-church. Resources are put to optimal use by an organization that is positioned to carry out the mission more efficiently. The micro-church is able to concentrate on activities at which their members excel by providing funding or other resources that are utilized by the larger mission.

Acting as a volunteer force that assists an organization or multiple organizations to achieve their mission is also a very efficient mission model. Partnerships are established with these typically larger organizations that utilize the capacity of the micro-church very efficiently. The rewards and relative accomplishments produced from volunteering can outweigh having to organize and manage an in-house mission.

Churches come up with new ways to help people all the time. Some can bridge the gap between direct and indirect delivery by melding the two approaches. This may involve providing a niche service for another organization so that they can concentrate on a larger closely-related mission.

Micro-churches should be as creative as possible when designing a mission. Find the best delivery method available to carry out God's plan for the church. Constantly look for ways to improve or reinvent a mission to make it better. The ultimate challenge is to maximize the impact of the efforts put forward by the church to further the Kingdom of God.

TOOL 35: Mission Delivery Method Worksheet—*Identifies the methods to be used to deliver services to the people assisted by the mission.*

Capacity

Matching the size of the mission to the capacity of the church is very important. The scope of the mission needs to be sized so that the small micro-church can act within its designed capacity. Burdening members with an overly-challenging mission can be avoided if the mission properly utilizes the available capacity of the church.

Capacity is partly determined by the time that each member has to devote to the mission. A micro-church with members who work full-time and are raising families will not be able to devote as many hours to the mission as a church comprised of mainly retired individuals who are ready to dedicate their lives completely to Christ.

Take into account the immediate and planned membership levels when quantifying capacity. Determine the average time that identified members will be able to devote to mission activities. Use this average for any vacant positions to determine the total capacity of the church.

Consider the potential capacity that partnerships can add to the mission. A shared mission can multiply the human resources available to achieve the planned objectives. Volunteers can exponentially increase the manpower accessible to the mission. Consider all of these possibilities when determining the capacity of the mission.

The other component of capacity deals with the availability of the resources that are needed to accomplish the mission. Each mission has different resource requirements and opportunities. The way in which a mission is designed can increase or decrease the demand for material goods. Extensive resource requirements can severely limit a mission or make it unviable.

Optimizing the use of resources helps the church to hone in on what the actual mission should be. Eliminate waste by identifying the most efficient delivery system to carry out the mission. Look for opportunities where the same result can be achieved with fewer resources.

Outside resources will be required when internal resources are not adequate to carry out the mission. These resources may come from partners, other organizations, or individuals. Fundraising may also be needed to compensate for shortfalls in required resources. Designing the most economical delivery system will minimize the need for additional resources.

TOOL 36: Capacity Worksheet—*Identifies the human and physical resources that are available to the micro-church to achieve the mission.*

Inadequate Capacity

Temporary or permanent adjustments can be made to the mission to which the micro-church is being called, if inadequate capacity limits the church at any point in time. Joining another mission when the church is in the startup phase can be a temporary move until further capacity can be built up. The church can move forward with its own mission when adequate capacity is achieved.

The pace at which the micro-church sets out to accomplish the mission can be used to adjust for questionable capacity. Slowing the pace will allow the church to meet the objectives over a longer period of time while utilizing the available resources. The pace can also be throttled up and down to adjust for temporary fluctuations in capacity.

Consider designing the mission so that capacity is optimized by accelerating or decelerating the pace at which the objectives are approached. This will help to compensate for variations in membership levels as the church is being built or new churches are planted. It can also help with seasonal fluctuations that most missions experience.

The mission that the micro-church sets out to accomplish should not be diminished by limited thinking. Always look for ways to maximize the achievement of God's plan. Never underestimate God's power. Do not limit Him by settling for a mission that produces minimal accomplishments. Design the mission so that it has the best chance of achieving the desired objectives.

Delivery Mechanism

There are multiple ways for the micro-church to deliver the services being provided by the mission. A mechanism is a means by which a purpose is accomplished. The church needs to identify the specific mechanism that the mission will use to assist the target population and deliver a service to them.

Think long-term when identifying the mission mechanism. Missions are usually developed in stages that build upon each other. Develop a mechanism that can take the church through the process in stages as resources become available.

For example, the goal to start a soup kitchen may begin with members volunteering at an established soup kitchen where they can learn the ropes. The church can then graduate to a part-time mobile soup kitchen ministry. The ultimate goal can be realized when a permanent location is opened by creating partnerships with other organizations.

Each church needs to evaluate fully its calling and capacity and establish the best mechanism for fulfilling God's plan for the mission. The highest calling for a specific church may be to become the most outstanding volunteer force possible. Volunteering at the soup kitchen in the previous example may be the goal that a church is called to. Undertaking the calling with the highest level of commitment possible is what God is looking for.

TOOL 37: Mission Plan Template—*Summarizes all aspects of the mission and provides the framework within which the microchurch mission will operate.*

Chapter 20

Mission Promotion

"Make you perfect in every good work to do his will, working in you that which is wellpleasing in his sight, through Jesus Christ; to whom be glory for ever and ever. Amen." (Hebrews 13:21 KJV)

Promotion

A mission will start to build momentum once results are produced. Further resources and partnerships will need to be identified in order to sustain this momentum. Ongoing promotion will help to provide the resources required to keep the mission moving forward.

Donations or other resources that are required to support the mission should be identified during the design process when a funding model is being selected. The promotional methods used to tap into these resources need to be tailored to fit the specific mission. Promotional activity should be designed to keep resources constantly flowing.

Promotional Tools

Getting the word out generates awareness. Awareness generates resources and partnerships that can maximize the impact of the mission. Common promotional tools including websites, social media, and blogging can be used to help get attention. The micro-church will need to weigh the cost in member time and resources to use these tools. Many churches will add these tools gradually as the mission grows to minimize the drain on resources.

Websites can be created quickly and at minimal cost. This popular promotional tool can help the church get the word out about the mission and can also be used to accept donations. The work involved with creating and maintaining a website should not be overlooked when deciding whether to use one as a promotional tool. Identify the benefits of starting a website and decide whether they outweigh the costs in time and money before committing to build one.

Using social media has many of the same attributes as websites and may be more versatile for the micro-church. Platforms such as Facebook, Instagram, and YouTube can keep people informed and connected. These tools can also be used for promotional campaigns and donations. The downside of social media is the time it takes to create content and respond to others.

Missions usually require some type of social media presence to reach the desired audience. Starting slowly with one platform, such as Facebook, will help to determine the validity of social media as a promotional tool. Content must be added regularly to make these tools useful. Be prepared to devote the required resources needed to make social media a productive promotional device.

Blogging is another tool that can be used to get the word out. This activity is also very time-consuming. The benefits of blogging may not be apparent up front. A loyal following can be developed over a period of time that can be beneficial for small organizations. Churches should analyze the resource requirements of this activity and determine if enough value is received for the time invested.

Much of the content created for each of these promotional tools can also be posted on the other platforms with little or no modification. Every weapon used in the promotional arsenal should have fresh information that will motivate people to return and even contribute. This contribution can be in the form of funding, resources, volunteering, or partnerships.

Mission Promotion

TOOL 38: Promotion Worksheet—*Identifies the methods of promotion that will be used by the mission to create awareness and attract funding.*

Email Promotion

One tool that all micro-churches should incorporate into their promotional arsenal is the email campaign. Email addresses are a valuable resource for any organization. Micro-churches should obtain the email addresses of everyone that they come in contact with.

Targeted lists can be created to keep in contact with donors, volunteers, or partners. The time spent on managing these lists can be minimized with email marketing solutions, such as Constant Contact or Mail Chimp. Mail Chimp has a free option that can be used to see if this tool is beneficial for the mission. The costs of these services can be well worth it if substantial resources are needed to support the mission.

Design an email campaign plan that reaches the intended audience without overburdening them with emails. Include general emails that explain what the mission is, who is being helped, and how others can participate. The email campaign should take an indirect approach in the beginning. Gradually build the case that will compel the recipients to contribute.

Intake

Promotion may also be needed to identify participants who will be assisted by the mission. Many missions will not have an ongoing source of participants without actively seeking them out. Some missions may need to process a number of applicants before a target participant is identified.

An intake system should readily identify participants, so they are available when the mission is ready to help them. Missions that help a lot of people will need to have an intake system in place before the mission is launched. If possible, start a waiting list of potential participants who have been identified from previous activities.

Establish an intake system that produces qualified participants. Look for other organizations undertaking similar missions that may be overwhelmed. These participants are typically pre-qualified and may fit the mission's requirements. Partner with these organizations so that a flow of participants can be established.

Telling the Story

A micro-church needs to be able to tell the story about the accomplishments that God has achieved through the church and mission. Good testimony motivates people to act and makes it easier to promote God's agenda. Developing stories about people who are helped through the ministry or about members who were transformed as a result of the church will motivate people to join the church or donate time and money.

The testimonial documentation process starts by gathering information in various formats, including written, photographic, audio, and video. Make a habit of automatically compiling information about each life changed as a result of the ministry. Turn each transformation into a motivational story that can be used for God's glory.

Chronicling the activities and triumphs of the micro-church community should also be an ongoing process. Telling the community's story will help to validate God's work within the micro-church. Testimony can be a powerful tool in leading others to Christ.

Give God thanks and praise for what has been achieved through Him. Celebrate the success that has been produced from the hard work of members and partners. Each person associated

Mission Promotion

with the mission needs to know how much their help is appreciated.

"And whatsoever ye do in word or deed, do all in the name of the Lord Jesus, giving thanks to God and the Father by him." (Colossians 3:17 KJV)

CHAPTER 21

Startup Process

"Finally, my brethren, be strong in the Lord, and in the power of his might." *(Ephesians 6:10 KJV)*

Startup Phasing

Micro-churches can easily be overwhelmed by attempting to launch multiple elements of the church simultaneously. The church, mission, and network all require the full attention of the members before being set into motion. A phased startup avoids issues that can get the church off to a poor start.

The church itself should be on solid ground before launching further activities. The best approach is to start building the micro-church community around the worship service. Even the service can be phased so that components, such as the meal and Communion, can be gradually added to ensure that the community is focused on establishing the relationships upon which everything else will be based.

It may take several months for the nucleus of the community to be formed around this weekly gathering. Use this time to grow and plan. The other components of the church are often in the planning stages during this time period.

Mission and network activities are usually interrelated. Partnerships may need to be established before the mission can be launched. Resources required for the mission must also be identified and accumulated before the startup. This may involve an additional fundraising phase that will provide the initial resources for the mission.

Phasing the activities related to the mission in a planned and organized manner allows for evaluation of each element as it is launched. Any required changes can be implemented prior to moving forward with a new element. The church is able to establish momentum that can then be carried over into the next phase being launched. The object is to keep moving forward at a constant pace without overloading the members.

The four major elements of the micro-church include the church, mission, network, and the planting of new churches. Each of these elements needs to be broken down into sub-elements that are small enough to be easily accomplished. The phasing process then places each sub-element into the order that it should be accomplished.

TOOL 39: Startup Phasing Worksheet—*Determines how the various aspects of the church and mission will be phased during the startup process.*

Launch Time?

The formal launch of the micro-church is an exciting and important time. Making sure that the path ahead is clearly defined by completing the tasks outlined in this book will lead to a successful launch. Let's review what it will take to launch a new micro-church confidently.

Asking God for permission to launch should be just a formality at this point. Members have been receiving confirmation throughout the process, as an open line of communication with God was established through prayer and interaction with the Holy Spirit. One final affirmation is in order to enlist the continued support of the Holy Spirit.

A church is considered to be in the startup phase for the first year of its existence. Many of the foundational components of the church will need to be identified up front and then completed over this time period. Establishing a network and planting a new church are components that can typically take up to three years to complete.

Startup Process

The church needs to know where it is going and how it is going to get there. Planning should be as complete as possible before the launch date. Having a well-thought-out plan will help to propel the church in the right direction. The following are some of the tasks that should be complete while preparing to launch the church:

- Received divine revelation that the church is in God's plan.
- Identified the core members of the church.
- Determined the purpose of the church and mission.
- Defined target demographics and membership size.
- Designated the required roles and leadership positions.
- Selected a spiritual leader or team.
- Set goals and objectives that will help to fulfill the purpose of the church and mission.
- Engaged other potential church members.
- Started establishing the framework for the community.
- Identified the spiritual path for member maturity.
- Formatted the worship service and established a schedule.
- Determined the logistics of the shared meal.
- Established and evaluated the venue(s) that will be used.
- Designated the modes of communication to be utilized.
- Defined the mission and how it will be phased over time.
- Determined the financial resources needed to support the church and mission.
- Identified the sources of the required resources.
- Identified partners that can fill the initial gaps in capacity.
- Defined the network structure that will be formed or joined.
- Identified how new churches will be planted and set a tentative schedule.
- Started identifying core beliefs of the church.

- Established an evaluation system to monitor results.
- Set up a system to document activities.

Pre-Launch Meetings

A series of pre-launch meetings should be scheduled to finalize the plan of action and to remind each person of their roles. Members and partners need to be clear as to the purpose of the church and how the established goals will be achieved. Details of the decisions that were made during the planning stage should be communicated to all members. They need to have a clear understanding of how and why the decisions were made.

Members should identify further planning activities during the initial meeting. Create a to-do list of actions that need to be taken prior to the church launch. This list should be prioritized so that the most important items can be tackled first. Decide who will complete each item and communicate these responsibilities. Keep the list up-to-date so that it is clear at any point in time what needs to be completed before the launch.

The pre-launch meetings are used to motivate and energize the participants. Members should be primed and ready to execute the plan when the launch takes place. This may mean that some members need to take time before the launch to set new priorities in their lives that are in line with the church objectives.

Each person needs to be ready to commit the time and effort to make the church a success. Any issues should be addressed and solutions identified before launching. It is important that each member is ready for the challenges ahead. Take the necessary time to make sure that all members are on the same page and ready to move forward.

Momentum

The church should begin to gain momentum as each new sub-element is put into motion. The growth that results from this momentum needs to be sustained throughout the life of the

Startup Process

church. This continued growth will ensure that goals are achieved and objectives are reached. Too many micro-churches lose this initial momentum and never regain it.

Monitoring progress is the key to ensuring that this growth is ongoing. The next chapter will delve into establishing a monitoring plan that will help to identify issues quickly. Solving problems in a timely manner will help the micro-church to minimize the consequences that are produced.

Ongoing planning is another key to sustaining momentum. The evaluation process should identify areas that need improvement. More formal planning may be required when these adjustments are major enough to change potentially the direction of the church. Any changes that are implemented should be designed to have minimal effect on the momentum that the church and mission have established.

The enemy is always seeking to steal, kill, and destroy. Satan works constantly to make inroads into the Christian community and believers' lives. A well-planned micro-church with sustained momentum will be able to break through this opposition. Make sure that members are motivated to fight when the battle comes.

"The thief cometh not, but for to steal, and to kill, and to destroy: I am come that they might have life, and that they might have it more abundantly." (John 10:10 KJV)

CHAPTER 22

Progress Evaluation

"Prove all things; hold fast that which is good." (1 Thessalonians 5:21 KJV)

Taking the Pulse

Evaluation is integral to the success of any organization. Monitoring key aspects of the micro-church and mission is essential for ensuring that progress is being made toward the planned objectives. Mistakes made early in a process can amplify over time and become major issues. Reacting quickly when issues arise usually minimizes the severity of the repercussions that affect the church.

An evaluation system should be established as the micro-church is being planned and launched. Consistently monitoring developments helps to identify the necessary changes to keep the church and mission on course. One or more members should be assigned to take the pulse of the organization on an ongoing basis.

TOOL 40: Monitoring Plan Template—*Identifies an evaluation system that can be used to keep the church and mission on track.*

Change

Change is inevitable in all aspects of life. Positive change should be embraced as a pathway to improvement. A need for change may be God's way of telling the micro-church that it is time to execute a course correction. Spiritually-inspired change sets the stage for continual advancement of God's plan by the church. Using the Holy Spirit as the inspiration for change ensures that the right path is followed.

One of the key advantages of a monitoring system is being able to recognize the need for change before issues begin to appear. Not recognizing obstacles early in the process limits the options available to deal with them. Avenues of change also become more difficult when an issue fully manifests.

Solutions to issues cannot be pinpointed until there is an understanding of why change is required. Jumping to a quick conclusion usually results in a poor decision being made. Micro-church members should evaluate the root cause of an issue before identifying potential solutions. Determine the best solution after fully vetting the issue.

Detailing the exact actions that are required to make the change will provide a direct path to obtaining the expected results. Obstacles that can prevent the change from being carried out need to be identified and removed as part of the process.

When a change is implemented, it should be monitored to confirm that the planned results are achieved. The change management process is an ongoing process that is integral to the evaluation system. Setting goals around the changes will help to keep them in the spotlight.

Community Health

The health of the micro-church community requires constant monitoring. Taking swift action to deal with any interpersonal issues that arise will ensure that the community continues to thrive and grow in a positive manner. Of utmost importance is building and maintaining a sacred community where each member is cherished.

Having input is important for most micro-church members. Everyone wants the church to be successful and to thrive. Being open to making changes that improve the community is a commitment that each member should embrace.

Leaders need to receive feedback regarding their performance, whether it is good or bad. Establish two-way communication by providing comments and suggestions on an ongoing basis. This allows the leaders to grow and better manage their responsibilities. Constructive criticism is invaluable but should be delivered in a tactful manner.

A spiritual leader needs feedback as to the effectiveness of their spiritual guidance. Ideas for improvement should be solicited by the leader on a regular basis. Sincere positive feedback can inspire the leader to stretch even further to help the members discover new revelations.

Capturing Information

Reliable data is needed to evaluate results and make necessary changes. Information gathering typically does not occur until there is a specific need, which is typically after the fact. Backtracking and a lot of effort are usually required to mine the data being sought, if it still exists.

Identifying the information needs up front will allow the micro-church to capture the necessary data and make it available in a timely manner. Churches need this valuable information for various reasons including:

- Establishing credibility.
- Analyzing goal achievement.
- Making decisions.
- Attracting donors.
- Motivating members and volunteers.

Spreadsheets make it simple for churches to collect data. A database should be considered if there are extensive records being collected. Identifying the information requirements up front distinguishes what data is valuable. Creating a system to capture this information will ensure that this valuable data is collected.

Useful Information

Other types of information should be gathered and stored as background data that could be useful for future decision making. This is typically information that can be used to track the various activities of the micro-church. Looking back at previous actions can provide invaluable knowledge that helps to avoid future mistakes.

Tracking the spiritual path of the church is important to eliminate redundancy or identify gaps in spiritual knowledge that need to be filled. A long-term study plan should be created and used to guide the church through the maturity process.

The spiritual path may need to be redirected as the church evolves. Adjustments will also be needed as new members join the church. Capturing the background information that documents what knowledge has been gained will make this task easier.

Revelations received from the Word should be preserved and incorporated into the statement of faith, when appropriate. Documenting these godsends will help each member to mature in Christ. One revelation will often lead to further revelations. The Scriptures and the decision-making process that precipitated these revelations should be archived.

Outreach efforts should be tracked to determine what techniques work the best. The results can help to refine the outreach approach and increase its effectiveness. The outreach plan designed during the micro-church startup period should be modified as these refinements are made. Archiving the background information related to these changes may help to spark additional ideas in the future.

Personal information, such as name, address, email, phone number, birthdate, and anniversary date, should be gathered as members join the church. Collecting this data up front will ensure that the church has it available when needed. A member profile can be created to store this information and other member background information.

TOOL 41: Member Profile—*Gathers key information about each member.*

Partner contact information should also be gathered as each relationship is being established. Document any formal agreements that have been made or other arrangements that have been verbalized. Notes that will capture key information about potential partnerships that were previously explored may be invaluable in the future.

Each micro-church will have different information gathering needs. Ensuring that valuable information is captured is what is important. How the information will be used is what determines its value. Carefully strategize what information should be retained and set up a system to capture and store it.

Make sure that the information being collected has value. Saving everything can create more of a burden than it is worth. Establish rules for record retention that make sense. Don't waste valuable member time that in the end will not produce anything of value.

TOOL 42: Record Retention Worksheet—*Identifies what information needs to be gathered and how it is to be retained.*

Required Data

Some data is required to be tracked for legal and financial purposes. The legal structure of the church or mission will dictate what these requirements are. An unincorporated association will have far fewer requirements than a non-profit organization.

Even the unincorporated association should keep minimal records to document activities. The church may have to prove its unincorporated status at some point in time. This initial legal structure may also be abandoned in the future for a structure that provides needed protection as the church grows.

The church should consider forming a formal legal structure up front if an extensive mission will be launched that will require this move at a later date. A more extensive record keeping system should be set up initially, if the church plans to form a non-profit or other legal entity in the future. This will ensure that all pertinent data is captured. When the switch takes place, there is no need for backtracking.

Automating wherever possible will save time and ensure that information is secured before it is lost. Use computer software to capture data in a uniform fashion. Programs, such as Quicken, can store financial data and provide important reports that can be beneficial for planning.

Micro-churches need to set up an information handling system that details how data will be captured, processed, and stored. Key persons should be assigned responsibility to handle the information that is gathered and secure it for processing. Guidelines should be set up for processing and storing the data on a regular basis.

Important information should be backed up on multiple systems. Electronic data can be stored on a computer, a backup drive, portable drives, and online. Make sure that the data is secure and easily accessible when the intended audience needs it.

CHAPTER 23
Averting Mistakes

"And be not conformed to this world: but be ye transformed by the renewing of your mind, that ye may prove what is that good, and acceptable, and perfect, will of God." (Romans 12:2 KJV)

Missteps

Missteps can have a much greater effect on the micro-church than with other organizations or traditional churches. Issues can become amplified within the smaller church environment and thus have relatively greater consequences. Errors need to be corrected quickly to minimize the damage.

The evaluation system described in the previous chapter is an early warning system that helps to avoid or minimize mistakes once the church has been launched. It is also important to spend time evaluating potential risks during the design stages of the church and mission to identify pitfalls that can be avoided. Design miscalculations can substantially hinder the planned objectives as the church grows.

Engaging other micro-churches or organizations that are similar in design can provide great insight. Gaining wisdom through the lessons that others have learned can help the church to avoid many of the stumbling blocks that can lead to issues. The time used for the discovery process is well spent considering the potentially wasted effort resulting from major missteps.

Failure Reasons

It does not take too much to make a church fail other than doing the wrong thing for an extended period of time. Much is at stake when traditional churches fail. The failure of a smaller micro-church may not be of the same magnitude, but it can set back God's plan and devastate the people involved with the church.

Failure should not be an option. It certainly will not be the result if the Holy Spirit is in the forefront. Make sure that the church has received God's stamp of approval before getting too far into the process. Proceed with confidence once He has given the go-ahead. Follow His lead to ensure success.

The issues that cause churches to fail are often very clear to see early in the process. The problem is that leaders fail to recognize them and react with viable solutions. Some church congregations are still scratching their heads as they pull the plug. The following are potential concerns for micro-churches that can easily be avoided:

- Failing to plan and prepare.
- Selecting the wrong legal structure.
- Improperly sizing the membership.
- Not defining member demographics.
- Poorly designing the mission.
- Not networking with other churches and organizations.
- Not embracing the calling of the church.
- Not fulfilling the calling of church members.
- Not centering the church and mission on the Word.
- Neglecting to develop the community fully.
- Sabotaging the church by a misguided member.
- Engaging members who do not fit the unique community.
- Not sustaining the initial momentum.
- Not following the planned path.
- Not monitoring progress.

Success Traits

Successful micro-churches exhibit common traits. Designing these characteristics into a new church will help to eliminate the missteps that typically result from their absence. Each church will need to determine how these traits can be incorporated into their specific design. Traits that can ensure the success of a micro-church include keeping the church:

- Small
- Efficient
- Productive
- Moving forward
- Significant
- Focused on the Word
- Mission-oriented
- Centered on loving others
- Rewarding.

Meeting Resistance

Every micro-church will meet with resistance during its existence. Issues are inevitable for a church that is promoting the Kingdom of God. Satan and his minions will attack a successful church from all angles in an attempt to destroy what its members have achieved through God.

Be prepared to fight the battle when it comes. Know that God has the church's back and that He will have the tools in place to fight through the resistance when they are needed.

"Trust in the Lord with all thine heart; and lean not unto thine own understanding." (Proverbs 3:5 KJV)

There are typically preliminary signs that point to impending issues that can affect micro-churches. These signs will present themselves well before the problem surfaces. Recognizing these signs will enable the church to make the changes needed before small problems manifest into major issues. Some of these signs include:

- Reduction in church attendance.
- Drop in member enthusiasm.
- Decrease in membership size.

- Power struggles between members.
- Goals and objectives not being met.
- Increase in interpersonal struggles.
- A mission that has gone off course.
- A spiritual path that is not progressing.
- Partnerships that are floundering.
- Partners not meeting commitments.

Reacting appropriately to resistance when it occurs is the challenge that church members face. Anticipating a setback may not always be possible. Micro-church members should establish a mindset that any challenge can be overcome with God's help. This enables the church to react positively to challenges and gain the upper hand.

TOOL 43: Troubleshooting Process Worksheet—*Establishes the process to be used to resolve issues quickly.*

Crisis Management

The micro-church may find itself in a crisis situation at some point in its existence. Trouble may come from within the church or can result from outside factors. Swift action usually needs to take place when a crisis occurs.

Micro-churches need to be prepared to act, no matter what the source of controversy. Identifying protocols that can be followed when tragedy hits will set the church up for a quick recovery. Crisis management is basically a troubleshooting mechanism that is executed within an abbreviated time period.

Crisis management protocols can be created for internal emergencies, such as the death or injury of a member or the surfacing of a major mission roadblock. External factors, such as hurricanes, tornadoes, earthquakes, fires or world-wide terrorism threats, can impact the micro-church to a greater extent than the more manageable internal factors. Protocols can also help to reduce the effects of these unpredictable threats.

Being prepared to react may not resolve the crisis, but it will position the church to respond appropriately and with confidence. The severity of an emergency can be reduced through swift action and prayer.

Dispute Resolution

Disputes are inevitable within any organization. Setting up a process to deal swiftly with controversy when it arises will help to minimize the fallout. Don't let a miscommunication fester until relationships are damaged. Protect the micro-church community by being proactive whenever possible.

Some churches assign the responsibility of overseeing the activities of the community to one member. This person observes member interactions and takes action to preempt any disputes. This observer may also act as a referee when minor disputes occur.

The formal dispute resolution process should include a system that seeks to deal with an issue as soon as it presents itself. Members should be encouraged to terminate disputes before they escalate and to bring the underlying issue to the full membership if the situation warrants it.

Both sides of the issue should be presented in an open forum. All options for resolution should be discussed, and the best settlement should be endorsed by the group. Of prime importance is that the parties to the dispute are both on board and that there are no lingering issues or resentment.

CHAPTER 24

Network Building

"For if they fall, the one will lift up his fellow: but woe to him that is alone when he falleth; for he hath not another to help him up." (Ecclesiastes 4:10 KJV)

Networking

One of the most important activities that the micro-church can engage in is making connections with other individuals and organizations that will help to bring unity within the Body of Christ. Relationships can be used to empower the church and further the Kingdom of God. Many of these connections are required for a micro-church to be successful. Other associations can supercharge a church to receive supernatural prosperity that goes far beyond what could have been anticipated.

Operating in a silo is not an option for the small-scale micro-church. The limited capacity that results from being disconnected from other followers is not what God intended for this unique church model. The home-based churches identified in the Bible were all connected through relationships.

The networking goal should be to position the church and mission for maximum effectiveness in achieving God's plan, both for the micro-church and for the partner organizations and individuals. This can be accomplished by building the best network possible and optimizing the use of resources and relationships.

Most micro-churches do not have members who represent each of the fivefold ministries described in the Bible. These ministries include apostles, prophets, evangelists, pastors, and teachers. Few traditional churches have members who represent all of these vital ministries. The micro-church can gain access to all of these ministries by making strategic connections with other churches and ministries.

Many people are convinced that a great revival is now in its infancy. The micro-church revolution is poised to be a major mechanism that will be used to unite the Church. The network system that is being created will help to bring together all of the components of the Body of Christ.

Networking Stages

There are four basic networking stages which the micro-church will need to go through before a network can be fully developed. A fifth stage is discussed but not required by most churches. Network building is a constant process that takes place throughout the life of the church. Having a network strategy that is God-driven is important.

The <u>first stage</u> of network building is establishing the connections required to launch the micro-church successfully. These are the relationships that fill the gaps that the smaller micro-church experiences because of its size. First stage partnerships help initially to establish the church and to provide a platform upon which the full network can be expanded. Some partners that can help during the formation of the micro-church include:

- Traditional churches that can provide a venue for special events, such as weddings, funerals, or baptisms.
- Micro-churches that can serve as mentors for the startup church.
- Advisors who can provide business and legal advice.
- Sponsors that are needed to provide funding and other resources.
- Established micro-church networks that can be joined.

The <u>second stage</u> of network building forms partnerships that can help the micro-church launch their mission. These direct

Network Building

or indirect relationships help the church to connect with established missions or provide support for the in-house micro-church mission. These connections can take the form of:

- Churches or non-profits whose missions can be joined.
- Missions with related activities that can provide knowledge and support.
- Businesses that can provide services and support the mission.
- Ministries that can be supported by the micro-church.
- Volunteers who can help to expand the mission.

The third stage of the networking process provides the framework under which new churches will be planted. The micro-church will grow to a point where maximum member capacity is exceeded. A planting plan is developed prior to this time that enables the church to spin off a new church.

There are usually close relationships between planted churches and the original micro-church. Planted churches often share the philosophy, mission, and objectives of the original church. Each church acts independently, but common bonds allow them to perform as one unit within the Body of Christ.

Networking creates a combined capacity that produces economies of scale that can be enjoyed by each church involved. The churches can share volunteer groups for mission or fundraising events as well as other common functions. This enlarged capacity allows each church to accomplish more without expanding membership size.

The fourth stage of networking establishes relationships that can be used to increase the influence of the micro-church. The church should always be in an expansion mode once it is fully established. This stage allows the church to use the power of the network to expand exponentially and create connections that would not have previously been available.

A networked church is able to position itself to take advantage of unique opportunities, that will present themselves as a result of the relationships that have been established. God will send people or provide supernatural connections that can change the dynamic of the church. The micro-church needs to be open to these godsends and act on them when they are received.

The activities of the micro-church may eventually expand beyond the area of influence that was initially established by the church. The focus may spread from a single neighborhood to a city, county, state, or national level. This expansion can be achieved using the power and influence of a strategically-designed network.

A fifth stage of launching a formal network of micro-churches is one that not all churches will be called to. The main objective for these churches is to establish and support a wide network of churches. This network can be local, regional or national, depending on the focus of the church. These organizations also help to support the overall micro-church movement that is taking place around the world.

Phasing Relationships

Not all of the relationships that a micro-church plans to create can be established at the same time. Relationships take time and energy to develop and cultivate. The church can be launched with a handful of strategic partnerships, and other relationships can be phased in as time allows.

Don't get overwhelmed by trying to establish too many relationships at the same time. Network building is an activity that will be undertaken throughout the lifetime of the church. Partners should be strategically phased-in over time, as opportunities present themselves.

The partnerships that are formed as a network is being established can be with a variety of organizations as well as

Network Building

individuals. Taking advantage of as many types of partnerships as possible will help to create a balanced network that can grow exponentially. Relationships should be explored with diverse organizations including:

- Micro-churches
- Traditional churches
- Ministries
- Non-profits
- Community groups
- Christian businesses
- Other businesses
- Volunteers
- Donors
- Individuals.

These relationships can catapult a micro-church into a higher level of achievement. Every aspect of the church and mission should be analyzed to discover where synergies can be created through partnerships.

TOOL 44: Partner Evaluation Worksheet—*Evaluates network partners prior to committing to a relationship.*

Strategy

The micro-church should develop a networking strategy before any partners are identified and approached. Looking at the big picture will help to identify what partnership types are needed and at what point they should be integrated into the network.

Look for synergies that will enable the church to satisfy several needs within one partnership. For instance, a traditional church may be able to provide facilities for events, such as weddings and funerals, have a mission that the micro-church can join, and provide worship opportunities for celebrations, such as Easter and Christmas.

Every relationship that is explored should first be evaluated to determine if it fits the network strategy that is being developed. Gather as much information as possible about each organization being considered. This knowledge will help in the decision-making process.

The micro-church should also be exploring potential connections between network partners as relationships are being cultivated. Churches increase their potential for success by creating more connections. Evaluate the connections that each organization has established with their partners. Determine whether any of these organizations are a good fit for the micro-church.

TOOL 45: Networking Strategy Worksheet—*Provides a strategy for how network relationships will be created, phased, and expanded.*

Making Contact

Be prepared when approaching organizations as potential partners. Know exactly what the micro-church needs from the partnership and what it has to offer in return. Be able to give a detailed description of the church as well as outline the objectives of the mission. Identify potential benefits of the relationship before the first contact is made.

The first meeting should be used for exploration and relationship building. Subsequent meetings can discuss specific connections that will be beneficial for each partner. Continue to explore this relationship as other partners within this category are evaluated.

Always give before receiving from any relationship whenever possible. The micro-church needs to build trust and establish a reputation with every connection that it makes. Act with integrity in all actions that the church undertakes. Be supportive of each partner. Only promise what the church can deliver.

A seed should be planted with each contact that is made, whether or not the organization will eventually be used as a partner. These contacts may be of some help at a later date. The organization may be able to be used as a partner at another time as the mission evolves.

Objectives and goals should be created for each partnership that the micro-church establishes. Define exactly what is to be expected of each party and what results are anticipated. Each goal should be measurable so that the results can be quantified.

The objectives and goals should be monitored by both organizations. Regularly scheduled meetings will help to ensure that these partnerships are actively managed. Changes that enhance the relationship should be explored as they are identified.

Traditional Church Evaluation

One of the most important and productive connections that the micro-church can make is one with a traditional church. Larger churches can provide facilities, offer special worship experiences, become a mission partner, or facilitate connections with other organizations. Finding a proper fit for this important relationship is essential.

Micro-churches are typically located in an area where a variety of traditional churches can be evaluated for partnership opportunities. Narrow the pool by setting some basic parameters for the partnership. Each church should be evaluated and ranked using common criteria.

Most traditional churches have websites and a social media presence that can be used to gather the information necessary to evaluate them for potential partnership. General internet searches can also provide some answers. Complete this type of research before even considering the church as a partner. Then follow up by making contact with those churches that rank high on a prioritized list.

A micro-church may find it advantageous to forge partnerships with more than one traditional church. A single organization may not be able to offer all the resources that the micro-church needs. Be open to partnering with several traditional churches. There may be additional connections that can be made between these traditional churches that can benefit each organization.

TOOL 46: Traditional Church Evaluation Worksheet—*Evaluates traditional churches for potential partnership.*

Exploration Period

The micro-church may want to establish a trial period in which the partnership can be explored. This allows both parties to evaluate the relationship before fully committing. The exploration period may be for a specific event or may last for several months. The complexity of the relationship will typically dictate how long the period is.

Make sure that the relationship is explored thoroughly before the full commitment is made. Meeting resistance early on in the trial period may be a sign that the partnership needs to be analyzed further. It may also indicate that the relationship is not what God intended for the micro-church.

The exploration period needs to have a distinct ending period. A formal commitment should be established at some point or the relationship should be terminated. Reviewing the results of this trial period may lead to changes that can be implemented as the partnership is officially rolled out.

Relationship Management

A formal relationship needs to be managed once it is established. Ongoing review of all relationships will help to determine whether the partnerships are working properly, if they can be enhanced, or if the relationships need to be completely reevaluated. A formal monitoring system should be set up to ensure that these important partnerships are not neglected.

Micro-churches should be constantly searching for further connections that can be made through their established partnerships. Anything that can be done to establish beneficial relationships within the Body of Christ should be explored. These connections should include those that can benefit not only the church but their partners.

Network events can be staged to help build relationships with certain partners or the entire network. Events, such as social gatherings, outdoor activities, or outings, will allow the groups to bond. Closer bonds build stronger relationships that can benefit both partners.

Regular meetings should be established with key partners or partner groups. Always keep the lines of communication open and producing further connections. Be open to integrating new partners into the network as God sends them to the church.

Monitor network activities to ensure that all parties follow up with their commitments. Objectives and goals are used to ensure that the relationship is progressing. React quickly to any deviations from planned performance to ensure that relationships continue to grow.

TOOL 47: Partner Management Worksheet—*Details the planned network relationships and how they will be maintained.*

CHAPTER 25
Church Planting

"And he said unto them, Go ye into all the world, and preach the gospel to every creature." (Mark 16:15 KJV)

Church Growth

Limited membership size is the main disadvantage of the micro-church. It is inevitable that a church will grow beyond its designed capacity. The many advantages of the small intimate community are lost when this optimal capacity is exceeded. Planting a new church resolves the issue of growth while expanding the Kingdom of God.

Planting is the process of creating new churches. Planted churches act independently from the original church but usually remain closely aligned. The support and resources of the established church allow the new church to grow quickly and eventually plant churches of its own.

Some groups plant churches on a regular basis to manage their discipleship activities. These are usually churches that have direct discipleship as a primary mission. Their main purpose is to facilitate the movement of unbelievers through the process of salvation and maturity in Christ.

Planting involves starting a new church using the resources of the original church and then mentoring the new church for a period of time. The planted church has a built-in support network, which helps the members get up to speed quickly. The length of the mentorship will depend upon how well the planting leaders are trained. Planted churches are usually able to act on their own within a short period of time.

Many micro-churches use the design model created for the original church to plant a new church with minimal effort. Planting of a church includes many of the same activities as an original startup of a church. Common features can be easily adapted by the planted church. This reduces the startup requirements and automatically aligns the planted church with the established objectives of the original church.

Planting new churches can help to deal with the size limitations of the micro-church while multiplying the effectiveness of the mission. Planted churches often remain connected to the mission established by the original church. This relationship results in an expansion of mission activities that is extremely efficient and productive. The process creates new opportunities that can be used to achieve God's plan more fully.

Almost every micro-church is involved with the planting process at one time or another. Growth is inevitable if the church is answering God's calling. The advantages of planting new churches include:

- Overcrowding is resolved.
- New connections are created.
- Discipleship capabilities are expanded.
- Mission capacity is enlarged.
- Mission scope is widened.
- Network potential is broadened.
- Leaders are advanced.
- Fundraising opportunities are increased.
- Volunteer pool is expanded.
- Demographic issues can be resolved.

Planting Process

Micro-churches need to anticipate how growth will be handled over the lifetime of the church. Growth is unavoidable if God's plan is being followed. The planting process begins when

Church Planting

a church is formed. A planting plan is developed as part of the startup activities.

The planting plan enables members to project when a new church will need to be planted. It allows them to have all of the resources in place to carry out the planting when the conditions are right. The plan details the objectives, processes, and mechanisms needed for planting churches. Having this plan in place allows the church to act quickly when there is a need to plant a new church.

Planning also helps the church to get a jump start on the process of identifying and training the leaders who will plant the new church. A planting cannot occur until these leaders have minimal training. Training should be an ongoing activity so that planting leaders are available when needed.

The unique design of every micro-church makes the planting process different for each church. Well-networked churches are able to draw from partner organizations to plant churches more efficiently. New churches just starting to network will find the planting process more challenging.

The general planting process includes the following activities:

- Praying for guidance.
- Selecting a planting team.
- Developing a planting plan.
- Identifying the network structure.
- Setting goals and objectives.
- Identifying potential planting leaders.
- Selecting the planting leaders.
- Training the planting leaders.
- Choosing a venue.
- Monitoring membership levels.
- Identifying required resources.

- Obtaining the resources.
- Making the decision to plant.
- Recruiting new members for both churches.
- Initiating the planting.
- Providing mentorship.
- Networking the churches.

Planting a church oftentimes affects the momentum of the original church as critical members leave the group to start the new church. The key to a truly successful plant is minimizing this loss of momentum while jump-starting the momentum of the new church. Much of this success will come from the ability to recruit and to assimilate new members into both churches during this expansion period.

Micro-churches should develop a detailed checklist to ensure that all aspects of the planting process are covered each time a new church is launched. The process will become more efficient as the checklist is refined during each planting. A debrief after each planting will help to identify ongoing issues and find resolutions.

TOOL 48: Planting Checklist—*Lists the steps needed to plant a new micro-church.*

Planting Team

Several individuals should be assigned responsibility for coordinating the planting function of the micro-church. The planting team is assembled during the startup phase of the original church when the planting plan is being developed. This team may float back and forth between the two churches for a period of time while the new church is first being established. However, the team remains as members of the original church to coordinate all future planting activities.

There will be an ongoing relationship between the two churches if they are networked and share a common mission.

The planting team can help to coordinate these relationships during the startup period until the planted church is fully functional.

The planting team acts as ongoing mentors for the planted church once it is fully functional. Team members are available to answer questions and to help resolve issues. All of the churches within a micro-church network offer help wherever it is needed.

Planting Leaders

Planting leaders are those members who take on the responsibility of starting the new church. These leaders typically become the core members of the planted church and are instrumental in the design of the church and the spiritual leadership of the members. These founding members many times offer their homes as the main venue for the new church.

Planting leaders should be identified as early in the process as possible so that any necessary training can be completed. Setting the new church up with properly trained people and resources will help to avoid many of the typical planting challenges that can start a church off on the wrong foot.

Training of planting leaders is a process that the entire micro-church can participate in. Ongoing training ensures that a steady flow of leaders is available for future plantings. Goals should be created to ensure that the leaders are up to speed when a planting is anticipated.

The planting operation may have to be delayed if planting leaders are not prepared when a planting is indicated. Prematurely launching the church can cause issues for both churches that could have been prevented with proper planning. It is always better to wait until both churches are prepared for the planting.

Minimal training and experience requirements can be established for those called to plant a church. Experienced leaders in all areas of micro-church administration can begin mentoring planting leaders as soon as they are identified. Churches with frequent planting objectives should develop a formal training program for consistency.

Connections

Planting activities help to develop new connections and strengthen existing relationships. Of prime importance when planting a church are the relationships between the two churches and any network that has been established by the planting church. Carefully planning these strategic connections with an eye towards efficiency will help to maximize the effectiveness of each organization involved.

Potential interactions between churches should be examined as part of the planting process. Look for specific functions that can be consolidated or shared by the churches if there is a common mission. Eliminate duplication of effort wherever possible.

External connections that can strengthen the network should also be examined. Any partnerships that have been established by the original church should be examined for possible affiliation with the planted church. Look for new partnerships that can benefit both churches as part of this process.

Potential conflicts between these relationships should also be investigated as these connections are being examined. Relationships should make sense, be beneficial to both parties, and add to the ultimate objective of advancing the Kingdom of God. Pass on relationships that do not help to fulfill the purpose of the church.

Failure to network limits God's ability to work through a church. All micro-churches should form or join a network to enhance their ability to carry out His objectives. Planted churches are the backbone of this network. The relationships created by the planting process strengthen as the network grows and expands.

Strengthening Relations

Members often enjoy fellowship and outside activities with network affiliates formed through planting. Many networks schedule regular system-wide events where several or all of the closely-related micro-churches gather. These gatherings can take the form of a worship service, volunteer event, fund raising event, or a fun activity that creates bonds between the participants.

Any activity that brings planted churches together and builds relationships should be considered, including leadership meetings. Spiritual leaders may gather on a regular basis to compare notes and encourage each other. Mission leaders may meet to fine tune relationships and plan upcoming events. The potential for accomplishing the shared objectives is increased as more productive relationships are created within the network.

Relationships with other types of partners, such as traditional churches, non-profits, or Christian businesses, should also be cultivated. These partnerships may support the underlying micro-church network or can be a vital component of the mission and other activities undertaken by the church. Planned activities also help to build these relationships and create additional connections that benefit the entire network.

Planting Frequency

The planting process is usually triggered when church membership size exceeds a predetermined maximum level and stays above that threshold for a period of time. The target membership range is set during the planning stages of the church around limitations that are inherent in the micro-church platform, such as the size of the venue. This target is the range within which the membership is expected to fluctuate under normal circumstances.

The frequency at which churches are planted is unique to each micro-church. Some may go for years without planting a church. Others are called to a church planting ministry as a mission and may reproduce every four to six months or less. The average micro-church probably plants a new church every one to two years.

Many churches will set goals to plant new churches at a given frequency. This forces the church to focus on the actions necessary to prepare for the planting. They are prepared to plant a church when the timing is right, whether or not the target date of the goal is achieved.

The planting goal does not need to have a set date for the actual planting. The church will encounter many changes as it grows from a startup to a fledgling planter. It is best to work towards a planting rather than be controlled by a defined deadline.

Churches can identify the processes required to plant a church and the order in which each should be accomplished. Goals can then be set around completing each process within a specific period of time.

The planting frequency is not as important as being prepared when the need arises. God will provide the opportunity to plant a church when the conditions are right for both churches. He will put the people in place who will start the new church and oversee the process.

Planting Stages

Micro-churches will go through several stages in the process of planting a church. Planting operations should be kept in the

Church Planting

forefront at all times. The key to a successful launch of a new church is being prepared and ready to act when God moves.

The first stage of the planting process is pre-planning. A planting plan detailing all aspects of the process is created well before the need for expansion occurs. This plan is reviewed and refined on a regular basis so that it remains up to date and ready to execute with little notice.

Micro-churches within an established network should be consulted as part of the planning process. The planting efforts of churches within a network can be phased or staggered to minimize the impact on the network and to meet the needs of each church involved most effectively.

Recruitment is the second stage of the planting process. Planting leaders will be leaving the original church to start the new church. Additional members will be needed to fill the gaps in the memberships of both churches.

Starting the recruitment process prior to planting the new church will help to minimize any loss of momentum for the original church. The planted church will also benefit from this jump start by identifying additional members to bring the participation level up to the target membership range. Recruitment activities will continue until each church reaches a point where normal growth patterns can resume.

The third stage of the planting process is the actual planting of the church. This action is triggered when conditions for launching the new church are nearing fruition. The planting of a new church begins when all members are prepared and resources are in place. The decision is made to go ahead with the official launch when final preparations are complete.

The fourth stage of planting is mentorship. Planted churches need to be mentored until they are fully developed. Mentors can be recruited from the planting church or from other churches or organizations within the established network. Any resource that can be used to gain the knowledge and wisdom needed to lead the new church with confidence should be engaged.

Mentorship should be an ongoing process within micro-church networks. All churches need to share what they learn so that other churches can benefit from positive or negative experiences. The goal should be to make each church as efficient and productive as possible in advancing the Kingdom of God.

Multi-Church Planting

One of the benefits of networking is the ability to consolidate certain activities within a group of closely associated churches. One process that can be combined across multiple churches is planting. Churches are able to pull the people and resources needed for a planting from multiple churches, instead of each church waiting for the right conditions to be in place to plant churches individually.

This approach makes the planting process easier and more efficient. Little momentum is lost by the planting churches with the planting leaders and initial members being pulled from several established churches. The new church is well-positioned for a quick startup.

This approach requires planning by all participating micro-churches in the network. A network planting plan combines the objectives of the individual churches and acts as a master plan for the united effort. Regular communication is required to monitor the planting status at each church and act when the conditions are right.

Implanting

It may be beneficial for a micro-church to create a subgroup within the church that accommodates certain members with shared characteristics. This process is known as implanting a

Church Planting

church. The subgroup does not stand alone as a separate church but enjoys the benefits and resources of the main church.

This implanted group meets separately for the weekly service and Bible study, but it comes together with the church for participation in the mission, the shared meal, and other activities. An example would be a family-oriented micro-church implanting a church that caters to a specific age group, such as young adults. Their separate church service and Bible study would be overseen by adult leaders serving as mentors to the group.

This young-adult implanted church may complement the established mission of the main church by helping those in their age group. They may also develop a niche mission that can be very effective in addressing groups that the main church is not positioned to help. Give them the reins and be amazed at what happens.

TOOL 49: Planting Plan Template—*Details the process of planting a new church and sets goals and timelines.*

CHAPTER 26

Revolution Ahead

"And this gospel of the kingdom shall be preached in all the world for a witness unto all nations; and then shall the end come." (Matthew 24:14 KJV)

revolution (rev-e-loo-shen):

- "a sudden, complete or marked change in something" (Dictionary.com).
- "a fundamental change in the way of thinking about or visualizing something" (Merriam-Webster).
- "a sudden or momentous change in a situation" (The American Heritage Dictionary).
- "a complete or radical change of any kind" (Your Dictionary).
- "a drastic or far-reaching change in ways of thinking and behaving" (Definitions.net).

Momentous Change

God has big plans for the Body of Christ. It will be a <u>sudden momentous change</u> that will have <u>far-reaching</u> effects on <u>ways of thinking and behaving</u> of people around the world. A major awakening of the Church will include a fundamental shift in church platforms. The micro-church is positioned to play a key role in this game-changing move of God by being the catalyst for reconnecting millions of unchurched Christians.

Any revolution of God has one main purpose: to bring more people to Christ. Effective discipleship can only be accomplished if the Body of Christ is united and focused on this ultimate goal. The coming micro-church revolution will help to unite the Body of Christ in ways that have previously been unattainable.

Some would argue that this revolution has been underway for years. The groundwork that has taken place within the micro-church community since the 1960s has truly been a revolution. I believe that this is only the tip of the iceberg. God is planning to use this small church format to get the Church back to the simplicity of the 1st century church.

The Body of Christ is far from the unity that Christ seeks to bring it into. The revolution ahead will help to address this lack of unity. The micro-church is the best mechanism to spearhead the effort to unite all aspects of the Body of Christ. The model presented in this book maximizes the connections that will lead to this unity.

"I beseech you therefore, brethren, by the mercies of God, that ye present your bodies a living sacrifice, holy, acceptable unto God, which is your reasonable service. And be not conformed to this world: but be ye transformed by the renewing of your mind, that ye may prove what is that good, and acceptable, and perfect, will of God." (Romans 12:1-2 KJV)

Prophetic Consensus

Prophets around the world are prophesying about a coming move of God that will eclipse any other in history. I believe that God gave me this calling as part of His plan for a major revival of the Church. This is a revival that has already started. It is a revival that could even be tied to the second coming of Christ.

The micro-church will be one of the many tools that will bring about the changes that God is seeking. Unchurched Christians and other revolutionaries are shaping the way that this model will be used to help bring unity to the Body of Christ.

God is making moves that have astonished believers and unbelievers alike. The election of Donald Trump as president in 2016 shocked the entire world. Yet President Trump has already made some moves that only God could have orchestrated.

Trump's unilateral recognition of Jerusalem as the capital of Israel completely reversed the stance of previous administrations. This recognition is profound. It aligns the United States with God's chosen people. This sets the United States up for continued favor from God. God is using President Trump to position the United States to receive further blessings.

Prophetic declarations continue to be made and fulfilled. Believers need to prepare themselves for a move of God that will affect the entire world. Make your move now to engage with this revolutionary movement.

"For the prophecy came not in old time by the will of man: but holy men of God spake as they were moved by the Holy Ghost." (2 Peter 1:21 KJV)

Prioritizing Faith

Lives are being radically changed as people step into the revolution. The physical world is being deemphasized and the spiritual world is being embraced. Committed Christians are setting their priorities around faith rather than worldly pleasures. They are stepping out of the secular realm and stepping into the spiritual revolution--a revolution which provides them a full-time relationship with God through Jesus Christ.

These revolutionary Christians are embracing the plan that God has for their lives. They are breaking the bonds of religion that have held them captive for years. They are stepping out of legalism and into grace. They are praising God for sending Jesus to die for their sins rather than feeling condemned for their transgressions.

Building their faith is the number one priority of these revolutionaries as they discover God's plan for their lives and take positive steps towards achieving it. This revolutionary move is bringing about positive change that is based on the faith that

Christ compels each of us to have. A faith that comes from the absence of doubt.

"And Jesus answering saith unto them, Have faith in God. For verily I say unto you, That whosoever shall say unto this mountain, Be thou removed, and be thou cast into the sea; and shall not doubt in his heart, but shall believe that those things which he saith shall come to pass; he shall have whatsoever he saith." (Mark 11:22-23 KJV)

Revolutionary Leader

The revolutionary leader who has impacted the world more than any person has or ever will is Jesus. Jesus Christ's ministry only lasted three years, but the revolution that He sparked has lasted nearly 2,000 years. Most revolutions are marked by their brutality; His is expressed through absolute love.

His revolution started with the words "follow me." This continues to be the revolutionary call to all those who believe in Him. Make the choice to follow the ultimate revolutionary leader. All you need is faith.

"And Jesus, walking by the sea of Galilee, saw two brethren, Simon called Peter, and Andrew his brother, casting a net into the sea: for they were fishers. And he saith unto them, Follow me, and I will make you fishers of men. And they straightway left their nets, and followed him." (Matthew 4:18-20 KJV)

Commitment

Christ calls us to commit our lives to His supreme revolution--a revolution that will affect lives, not overthrow governments. It's a revolution that will provide everyone the opportunity to join and receive the incomparable love that is offered in return for commitment and faith.

The commitment level goes beyond a mere acceptance of Christ. He is looking for total commitment to His revolution. He wants to use each and every one of us to bring about change. His plan is simple, but powerful. His weapon is love--a love so intense that no one in their right mind can resist.

The micro-church offers the vehicle through which this commitment can be carried out. The strength in numbers that the church provides allows previously unconnected Christians to produce far more for Christ than could be accomplished on their own.

"A new commandment I give unto you, That ye love one another; as I have loved you, that ye also love one another. By this shall all men know that ye are my disciples, if ye have love one to another." (John 13:34-35 KJV)

Join the Revolution!

For those of you who are unsure about moving forward with this challenging venture, I would encourage you to follow God's lead. He will make it known to you whether you should pursue this form of church. If He has made His will known to you, I challenge you to move forward now. Don't wait for a convenient time. Step out in faith and pursue this calling with vigor. Be a part of the revolution ahead.

I encourage you to wholeheartedly consider joining the revolution. Explore what God has planned for you. Make a difference--a difference that promotes the Body of Christ for His glory. Be a part of the great movement of God that is happening. Take a leap of faith and join the revolution by starting a micro-church today.

Let me know how you are doing. Please contact me at rick@micro-churchrevolution.com. I look forward to hearing from you.

"For to me to live is Christ, and to die is gain." (Philippians 1:21 KJV)

APPENDIX

MICRO-CHURCH TOOL LIST

Tool 1: Micro-Church Startup Checklist—*Provides a detailed listing of the steps needed to start and grow a micro-church and track progress.*

TOOL 2: Common Feature Worksheet—*Identifies key features that can be incorporated into new micro-churches being designed.*

TOOL 3: Micro-Church Plan Template—*Presents the key components of micro-church design and summarizes the information obtained from the available worksheets.*

TOOL 4: Discovery Checklist—*Presents the steps necessary to perform the initial discovery process.*

TOOL 5: Startup Team Assessment Worksheet—*Evaluates the strengths and weaknesses of the team and identifies any major obstacles they may face when starting the church.*

TOOL 6: Spiritual Guidance Worksheet—*Identifies the methods used to seek spiritual guidance and ways in which revelations are received.*

TOOL 7: Mission Worksheet—*Defines the mission and the target population that the micro-church will be serving.*

TOOL 8: Purpose Statement Worksheet—*Creates an inspiring purpose statement that defines the calling of the church and its members.*

TOOL 9: Goal Summary List & TOOL 10: Goal Worksheet— *Help to define and track goals and objectives in all areas of micro-church development*

TOOL 11: Statement of Faith Worksheet—*Helps micro-church members through the process of creating an inspiring statement of faith.*

TOOL 12: Community Trait Checklist—*Identifies the shared traits that micro-church members will seek to develop over time.*

TOOL 13: Member Outreach Plan Template—*Creates an outreach plan that can be quickly executed when member outreach is required.*

TOOL 14: Communication Worksheet—*Identifies the best modes of communication for the church and mission.*

TOOL 15: Spiritual Path Plan Template—*Defines the spiritual path of the church and monitors the progress that is achieved.*

TOOL 16: Discipleship Plan Template—*Identifies the opportunities that the micro-church can provide to their members for discipling unbelievers.*

TOOL 17: Target Member Profile Worksheet—*Describes the ideal demographic characteristics in identifying new members.*

TOOL 18: Target Member Range Worksheet—*Sets limitations on membership size based on specific factors affecting the micro-church.*

TOOL 19: Member Tasking Worksheet—*Places members in the best church and mission roles to take advantage of their skills and interests.*

TOOL 20: Spiritual Leadership Worksheet—*Determines how spiritual leadership will be established and what resources will be needed.*

TOOL 21: Venue Analysis Worksheet—*Evaluates potential venues and selects the best option available to the micro-church.*

TOOL 22: Worship Service Template—*Helps to design the worship service and ensure that key service elements are included.*

TOOL 23: Bible Study Template—*Organizes the worship service teaching and documents subjects that have been covered.*

TOOL 24: Communion Service Template—*Assists with the design of the Communion service and the selection of related Scriptures.*

TOOL 25: Baptism Service Template—*Determines how baptisms will be handled and assists with the design of the service.*

TOOL 26: Meal Planner Template—*Organizes the shared meal and ensures that key elements of meal planning are incorporated.*

TOOL 27: Meal Signup Sheet Template—*Organizes each meal and serves as a reminder to the members of their contributions.*

TOOL 28: Meal Planning Tip Sheet—*Provides additional tips on planning the micro-church meal.*

Appendix

TOOL 29: Legal Structure and Liability Worksheet—*Explores legal structures that may make more sense for specific micro-churches and potential areas of liability.*

TOOL 30: Decision Process Steps—*Presents a typical decision-making process for use by the micro-church.*

TOOL 31: Decision Process Worksheet—*Provides a step-by-step worksheet for making decisions.*

TOOL 32: Mission Resource Worksheet—*Identifies the resources needed to undertake the micro-church mission and their potential sources.*

TOOL 33: Volunteer Utilization Worksheet—*Explores the potential for volunteers being used to expand the scope of the mission.*

TOOL 34: Fundraising Strategy Worksheet—*Establishes a strategy for raising the resources needed to fund the mission.*

TOOL 35: Mission Delivery Method Worksheet—*Identifies the methods to be used to deliver services to the people assisted by the mission.*

TOOL 36: Capacity Worksheet—*Identifies the human and physical resources that are available to the micro-church to achieve the mission.*

TOOL 37: Mission Plan Template—*Summarizes all aspects of the mission and provides the framework within which the micro-church mission will operate.*

TOOL 38: Promotion Worksheet—*Identifies the methods of promotion that will be used by the mission to create awareness and attract funding.*

TOOL 39: Startup Phasing Worksheet—*Determines how the various aspects of the church and mission will be phased during the startup process.*

TOOL 40: Monitoring Plan Template—*Identifies an evaluation system that can be used to keep the church and mission on track.*

TOOL 41: Member Profile—*Gathers key information about each member.*

TOOL 42: Record Retention Worksheet—*Identifies what information needs to be gathered and how it is to be retained.*

TOOL 43: Troubleshooting Process Worksheet—*Establishes the process to be used to resolve issues quickly.*

TOOL 44: Partner Evaluation Worksheet—*Evaluates network partners prior to committing to a relationship.*

TOOL 45: Networking Strategy Worksheet—*Provides a strategy for how network relationships will be created, phased, and expanded.*

TOOL 46: Traditional Church Evaluation Worksheet—*Evaluates traditional churches for potential partnership.*

TOOL 47: Partner Management Worksheet—*Details the planned network relationships and how they will be maintained.*

TOOL 48: Planting Checklist—*Lists the steps needed to plant a new micro-church.*

TOOL 49: Planting Plan Template—*Details the process of planting a new church and sets goals and timelines.*

NOW AVAILABLE!

MICRO-CHURCH TOOLBOX 2.0

Over 50 indispensable tools for starting and growing a micro-church:

- 7 Complete Plans
- 4 Comprehensive Checklists
- 29 Detailed Worksheets
- 6 Useful Templates
- 6 Administrative Tools
- Other Valuable Resources
- Free Product Updates.

This is a complete set of tools to get your micro-church up and running quickly. Save hundreds of hours of time with these efficient tools.

Start planning a micro-church today!

www.micro-churchrevolution.com/tools

Made in the USA
Middletown, DE
05 October 2021